**Reid Ewing and
Keith Bartholomew**

with
Dan Burden
Sara Zimmerman
Lauren Brown

Foreword by Janette Sadik-Khan

PEDESTRIAN-& TRANSIT-ORIENTED
design

 **Urban Land
Institute**

 APA

American Planning Association

Making Great Communities Happen

Recommended bibliographic listing:
Ewing, Reid, and Keith Bartholomew. *Pedestrian- and Transit-Oriented Design*. Washington, D.C.:
Urban Land Institute and American Planning Association, 2013.
ISBN 978-0-87420-201-4

Library of Congress Cataloging-in-Publication Data

Ewing, Reid H.
  Pedestrian- and transit-oriented design / Reid Ewing, Keith Bartholomew.
       pages cm
  Includes bibliographical references and index.
  ISBN 978-0-87420-201-4 (pbk.)
  1. Pedestrian traffic flow--Planning. 2. Urban transportation--Planning. 3. City planning. I. Bartholomew, Keith. II.
Title.
  HE336.P43E95 2013
  711'.74--dc23
                                    2013000739

About the Urban Land Institute

THE MISSION OF THE URBAN LAND INSTITUTE is to provide leadership in the responsible use of land and in creating and sustaining thriving communities worldwide. ULI is committed to

- Bringing together leaders from across the fields of real estate and land use policy to exchange best practices and serve community needs;
- Fostering collaboration within and beyond ULI's membership through mentoring, dialogue, and problem solving;
- Exploring issues of urbanization, conservation, regeneration, land use, capital formation, and sustainable development;
- Advancing land use policies and design practices that respect the uniqueness of both the built and natural environments;
- Sharing knowledge through education, applied research, publishing, and electronic media; and
- Sustaining a diverse global network of local practice and advisory efforts that address current and future challenges.

Established in 1936, the Institute today has nearly 30,000 members worldwide, representing the entire spectrum of the land use and development disciplines. ULI relies heavily on the experience of its members. It is through member involvement and information resources that ULI has been able to set standards of excellence in development practice. The Institute has long been recognized as one of the world's most respected and widely quoted sources of objective information on urban planning, growth, and development.

About the American Planning Association

THE AMERICAN PLANNING ASSOCIATION is an independent, nonprofit educational organization that provides leadership in the development of vital communities by advocating excellence in community planning, promoting education and citizen empowerment, and providing the tools and support necessary to meet the challenges of growth and change.

APA's more than 40,000 members include professional planners, officials, educators, students, and other individuals interested in making great communities happen. APA members can be found in all 50 states and in 75 countries.

Planners Press is APA's book imprint. It publishes titles of interest to practitioners, researchers, and the general public, with the aim of stimulating readers, creating an engaged citizenry, and influencing policy development. APA also publishes *Planning*, a monthly magazine; *Zoning Practice*, a monthly publication on local land use controls; the *Journal of the American Planning Association*, a quarterly journal; and *Planning & Environmental Law*, a monthly law journal.

Authors

Reid Ewing
Keith Bartholomew
with
Dan Burden
Sara Zimmerman
Lauren Brown

Project Staff

Gayle Berens
Senior Vice President, Education and Advisory Group

Adrienne Schmitz
Senior Director, Publications

James Mulligan
Managing Editor

Joanne Platt, Publications Professionals LLC
Manuscript Editor

Betsy VanBuskirk
Creative Director

John Hall Design Group
Cover and Book Design

Craig Chapman
Senior Director, Publishing Operations

About the Authors

REID EWING, PHD, is a professor of city and metropolitan planning at the University of Utah, associate editor of the *Journal of the American Planning Association*, and columnist for *Planning* magazine. Earlier in his career, he was director of the Voorhees Transportation Center at Rutgers University and associate professor at the National Center for Smart Growth. He served two terms in the Arizona legislature and worked on urban policy issues at the Congressional Budget Office.

Ewing has been studying the built environment and its effects on livability since the early 1990s. He has received several awards for his work over the years, including Best Article of the Year from the American Planning Association in 2010. His book *Best Development Practices* is listed by APA as one of the 100 essential planning books published over the past 100 years. He has published two previous books with the Urban Land Institute, *Developing Successful New Communities* and *Growing Cooler: The Evidence on Urban Development and Climate Change*.

Ewing holds master's degrees in engineering and city planning from Harvard University and a doctorate in urban planning and transportation systems from the Massachusetts Institute of Technology.

KEITH BARTHOLOMEW is an associate professor in the University of Utah's Department of City and Metropolitan Planning and is the associate dean of the College of Architecture and Planning. An environmental lawyer, Bartholomew served ten years as a staff attorney for 1000 Friends of Oregon and was the director of the LUTRAQ Project, a pioneering research program examining the interactive effects of land use development and travel patterns. With funding provided by the Federal Highway Administration, Bartholomew has studied scenario planning projects in more than 100 U.S. metropolitan areas, and the results from that research have been presented in many publications, including ULI's *Growing Cooler: The Evidence on Urban Development and Climate Change* (cowritten with Reid Ewing).

CONTENTS

APPENDIXES

Appendixes are available at www.lib.utah.edu/pedtransit.

Foreword

PEDESTRIAN- AND TRANSIT-ORIENTED DESIGN provides practitioners with a road map for building truly world-class cities. Reid Ewing and Keith Bartholomew have brought together research from across the field of urban design to give readers proven tools for creating healthier, stronger communities that will thrive in the 21st century.

Ewing and Bartholomew begin with a discussion of national polls on walkability. The bottom line is that a growing majority of Americans value places where they can walk to the corner store. People want to live in neighborhoods where walking and taking transit are safe and convenient, and they are voting with their feet. For cities, the question becomes, how can we build up these walkable neighborhoods near transit to meet demand?

City officials and planning practitioners can look to Ewing and Bartholomew's eight important qualities of urban design as the keys to the simple perception that a neighborhood is a great place to live and work. For example, research has shown that people prefer places that are *human scale* and have a sense of *enclosure*. These two principles alone can tell us a lot about the way we design streets and buildings.

These qualities do not translate to one-size-fits-all prescriptions. The 28 features of high-quality urban design described in the book provide a guide to some of the best concrete measures that cities can take. They cover most of the projects we have done in New York City in the last six years since the release of PlaNYC in 2007. We have created more than 23 high-quality public plazas on our city streets, realized the pedestrianization of Times Square and Herald Square, implemented a series of major pedestrian and bicycle improvement projects, and launched five Select Bus Service routes across the

city, with more under construction. We are also paying attention to the details. We are creating more places to sit to wait, whether at bus stops or along general sidewalks.

And New York is not the only city undertaking such projects. The members of the National Association of City Transportation Officials, which represent 15 of the largest cities in the nation, are building plazas, putting in new transit systems, and developing protected bicycle lanes all around the United States. The research that Ewing and Bartholomew have pulled together tells the story of why these projects are working.

At the end of the day, the best thing about the progress we have made is the safety and economic benefit that we have seen along with all of these projects. We have shown that we can make streets safe for people to walk, bicycle, and drive along, while meeting the needs of local businesses and residents and improving safety for all road users. This book is a valuable resource for planners, local officials, and others looking for ways to improve the pedestrian realm.

Janette Sadik-Khan
Commissioner
New York City Department of Transportation

President
National Association of City Transportation Officials

Preface

PEDESTRIAN- AND TRANSIT-ORIENTED DESIGN began its life in 1996 as a manual for the Florida Department of Transportation under the title *Pedestrian- and Transit-Friendly Design*. FDOT was making the transition, as many departments of transportation have, from being primarily a highway agency to being a multimodal transportation agency. The manual was based on the notion that great streets and great places require many complementary elements. The original publication identified 18 features that contribute to pedestrian- and transit-friendliness and classified them as essential, highly desirable, or worthwhile additions.

Much has changed in how communities are designed since the earliest version of the book, and this new, expanded version, published by the Urban Land Institute and the American Planning Association, reflects these changes. New urbanism has flourished, transit-oriented development has become commonplace, and smart growth has gone national. All three movements emphasize pedestrian- and transit-oriented design. The travel literature has expanded to include literally hundreds of studies showing that the "D variables" (density, diversity, and design) affect people's decisions to walk, bike, and use transit. Concerns over Americans' physical inactivity, obesity, and related chronic diseases have led to the active living movement and a rich literature demonstrating how important the built environment is as an influence on physical activity and weight status. Climate change has emerged as a national concern, having disappeared from the political landscape for a time, but now creating another imperative for reduced automobile dependence.

This book begins with a review of evidence showing that Americans value walkability. Chapter 2 describes the urban design qualities that make a place walkable, each a subtle combination of features that, in many cases, have been overlooked in the planning literature. As did the original FDOT book, chapters 3, 4, and 5 divide these features into three categories—essential, highly desirable, and worthwhile additions—and describe these features in detail. However, this new edition does much more. It expands the list of features to 28. It includes many new references. It provides dozens of progressive local code examples from around the United States. It grounds its recommendations in empirical evidence. And it provides a wealth of photographs and illustrations depicting design solutions, as well as failures.

We know that good urban design is more than the sum of these parts, but it helps us understand complex phenomena when items are classified, ranked, and dealt with individually as they are in this book. It is important to remember that the 28 elements have to be well integrated. With the copublication of this book by the leading organization of land developers, ULI, and the leading association of urban planners, APA, it is our hope that the reader will learn from and make use of its insights to make our communities that much better.

Reid Ewing and Keith Bartholomew
University of Utah

Acknowledgments

WE WOULD LIKE TO ACKNOWLEDGE THE CONTRIBUTIONS of our coauthors. Sara Zimmerman, senior staff attorney with the Public Health Law & Policy project prepared the feature boxes with code examples from around the United States. These examples move the reader from theory to practice. Dan Burden, executive director of the Walkable and Livable Communities Institute, is a noted authority on walkability and a leading photographer of urban scenes related to pedestrian-oriented design. Dan gave us over a million images to choose from. The book would be a shadow of itself without his photographic examples. Lauren Brown was an exceptionally able research assistant at the University of Utah. She was responsible for updating material and references from the original version of the book. Lauren is currently doing research and project development for Semilla Nueva, a nonprofit organization in Guatemala.

Equally important was the team at ULI. Adrienne Schmitz was the project director and substantive editor. She kept things organized and on schedule and managed others who worked on the book. Adrienne was a pleasure to work with. The copy editor was Joanne Platt, who worked very hard to correct grammar and ensure consistency throughout. Our very talented design consultant was John Hall. He designed the cover, book layout, and all the graphics. The authors are delighted with the look he has created. Finally, we want to thank Gayle Berens, who oversaw the contract and determined that this book would be published by ULI and the American Planning Association.

We could not ask for a better pedigree than ULI, which represents the land development community worldwide, and APA, which represents the urban planning community.

PEDESTRIAN- & TRANSIT-ORIENTED
design

CHAPTER 1

INTRODUCTION

THIS BOOK IS A HOW-TO MANUAL FOR CREATING GREAT PLACES that are walkable and transit oriented. It provides a mix of both the *subjective* and *objective* aspects of urban design and its role in creating walkable places, a key goal of smart growth. It begins with a discussion of the concepts espoused by the "founding fathers (and mothers)" of the urban design field, such giants as Gordon Cullen, Kevin Lynch, Jan Gehl, and Jane Jacobs. The book relies on hard data, such as consumer surveys, safety studies, and hedonic price studies. We find that the rhetoric of the great masters of urban design actually holds true in practice. Using both theory and data, we identify the most important aspects of urban design, explaining not only why good design matters but how it matters. Numerous photographs and drawings help support the assertions made and communicate ideas that are inherently visual.

This volume stands at the intersection of urban design and urban planning, leaning however toward urban design. Urban design differs from urban planning in scale, orientation, and treatment of space. The scale of design is primarily that of the street, sidewalk, park, or transit stop, as opposed to the larger region, community, or activity center. The orientation is aesthetic, as well as functional. The treatment of space in urban design is three-dimensional, with vertical elements being as important as horizontal elements in designing street space, park space, and other urban spaces. Urban planning, on the other hand, is customarily a two-dimensional activity (most plans, for example, are visually represented in *plan* view).

Building on work by the authors and others, this book ties together a rich urban design literature and empirical research in travel behavior, visual preference, real estate economics, and traffic safety.

This chapter provides an introduction to the topic. Chapter 2 outlines the urban design qualities that have been demonstrated to be central to pedestrian- and transit-oriented design. Chapters 3 through 5 follow with checklists of design features that would, ideally, be built into all transit-served areas. The features, which are illustrated with photos and graphics, fall into three classes: those deemed essential (chapter 3), those deemed highly desirable (chapter 4), and those deemed worthwhile but less essential (chapter 5). In a perfect world, all built

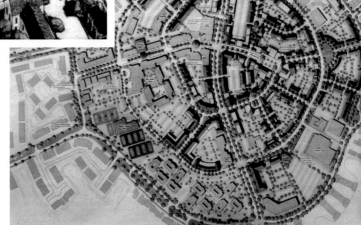

BELOW: **Large-scale, two-dimensional planning;** LEFT: **small-scale, three-dimensional design.** | *Dover, Kohl & Partners*

environments would contain all these features. But alas, the world is not perfect and the resources of local governments, transit operators, and developers in charge of building that environment are not limitless. Because choices must be made, some sense of priority is required.

The book concludes with chapter 6, which offers some recent examples of local policies and codes that address the needs of pedestrians and transit users.

Demand for Walkable, Transit-Oriented Development

THE DEMAND FOR WALKABLE, TRANSIT-ORIENTED DEVELOPMENT is growing. Perhaps the best national gauge of this demand is the National Survey on Communities, conducted for the National Association of Realtors in 2004 and 2011 (Belden Russonello & Stewart 2004, 2011). In this survey, respondents were given a choice between two communities labeled *A* and *B*. Community A was described as having single-family homes on large lots, no sidewalks, shopping and schools located a few miles away, and no public transportation. (The 2004 survey included commutes of more than 45 minutes.) In contrast, community B was described as having a mix of denser housing, sidewalks, shopping and schools within walking distance, and nearby public transportation (and in 2004, commutes of less than 45 minutes).

In 2004, 55 percent of those surveyed expressed a preference for community B, the smart growth community with a shorter commute. Of those who were thinking of buying a house within the next three years, community B appealed to 61 percent. Commuting time had a significant influence on respondents' preferences. About a third of the respondents said they would choose the smart growth design if commutes were comparable, while an additional quarter preferred such a design if it also meant being closer to work. By 2011, the percentage of

all respondents preferring the smart growth community had risen to 56 percent, and this without a commuting advantage.

Bolstering these results, a national consumer survey by the global public relations company Porter Novelli found that 59 percent of U.S. adults now support the development of compact, walkable communities.[1] Half would be interested in living in such communities (Handy et al. 2008). Levels of support were high among all groups except rural residents. More impressive than

FIGURE 1-1

Most Appealing Aspects of a Smart Growth Community

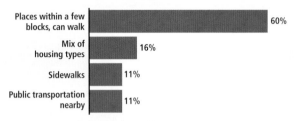

Places within a few blocks, can walk	60%
Mix of housing types	16%
Sidewalks	11%
Public transportation nearby	11%

Source: Belden Russonello & Stewart 2011, p. 24.

Note: The question, asked of people who had chosen to live in a smart growth community, was: "Look at the community you selected and choose the ONE most appealing characteristic of that community for you."

FIGURE 1-2

Americans Want to Walk More

Drive 55%

Walk More 41%

4% —Don't know/ refused to answer

Source: Belden Russonello & Stewart 2003.

Note: The question was, "Please tell me which of the following statements describes you more: A) If it were possible, I would like to walk more throughout the day either to get to specific places or for exercise, or B) I prefer to drive my car wherever I go."

the absolute levels of support was the increase in support between survey years 2003 and 2005, a statistically significant 15 percent, which the authors attribute to increased media attention on sprawl and its costs.

A third national survey, by the firm of Belden Russonello & Stewart (2003), found that 55 percent of Americans would drive less and walk more if they could. The survey question was, "Please tell me which of the following statements describes you more: A) If it were possible, I would like to walk more throughout the day either to get to specific places or for exercise, or B) I prefer to drive my car wherever I go." When asked for solutions to traffic congestion, 35 percent cited increased transit service, whereas 31 percent thought communities should be designed to shorten trips to work and shop. Only 25 percent thought the solution to traffic congestion lay in highway expansion.

There are regional surveys that reached conclusions similar to these national surveys (Levine and Frank 2007; Levine, Inam, and Torng 2005; Lewis and Baldassare 2010; Metz and Below 2011; Morrow-Jones, Irwin, and Rowe 2004). Lucy and Phillips (2006) note that "more respondents prefer compact, mixed-use, transit accessible developments than the percentage of such developments being constructed" (p. 237). As outlined in the next section, this gap between supply and demand will likely grow in the future.

A preference for walking over driving (Durham, North Carolina). | *Dan Burden*

Even More So in the Future

WHEN IT COMES TO HOUSING DEMAND, DEMOGRAPHICS ARE DESTINY. As baby boomers become empty nesters and retirees, they are exhibiting a preference for compact, walkable neighborhoods. These trends will likely accelerate because the baby boom generation represents America's largest generational cohort. By 2020, the number of individuals turning 65 years of age will skyrocket to more than 4 million per year. The Census Bureau estimates that between 2007 and 2050, the share of the U.S. population older than 65 will grow from 12.8 to 20.7 percent.

AARP (formerly the American Association of Retired Persons) has made transportation and quality-of-life matters among its top policy issues for the next decade. The organization is concerned because roughly one in five people over 65 does not drive at all, and more than half drive only occasionally (Bailey 2004). Older adults who lose their ability to drive remain at home most days, losing much of their independence and the ability to access essential services.

AARP surveys suggest that most people want to "age in place" (Bayer and Harper 2000). In most areas where older Americans are aging in place, alternatives to the automobile are limited. In fact, according to a national poll, only 45 percent of Americans over 65 live near public transportation (Mathew Greenwald & Associates 2003). The elderly are particularly inclined to walk when conditions are right. These findings, as well as the high cost of special transportation services, are reasons to make sure older people can easily access transit and live in safe, walkable communities.

Growth in households without children (including one-person households) will also affect living patterns dramatically. The percentage of households with children declined from 36 percent in 2000 to 33.5 percent in 2010. By 2025, only 28 percent of households will have children. Households without children are a natural market for urban living.

Beyond demographics, cultural changes are also at work in the housing market, particularly within generations X and Y, the two generations following the baby boomers. The children of the baby boom generation—referred to variously as echo boomers, millennials, and generation Y—have shown a preference for exciting, dense, urban places. A national study found that 57 percent of this cohort prefers small-lot housing and 53 percent values an easy walk from home to stores (Dittmar and Ohland 2004).

In 2011, a ULI survey of gen Y found 64 percent of respondents rated walkability "essential or preferable" (Lachman 2011). Results of the 2012 Home Design Trends Survey, conducted by the American Institute of Architects, are summarized by AIA chief economist Kermit Baker: "In many areas, we are seeing more interest in urban infill locations than in remote exurbs, which is having a pronounced shift in neighborhood design elements. And regardless of city or suburban dwellers, people are asking more from their communities in terms of access to public transit, walkable areas, and close proximity to job centers, retail options, and open space."

Most Americans prefer to age in place (West Hartford, Connecticut). | *Dan Burden*

FIGURE 1-3

Americans Want
to Age in Place

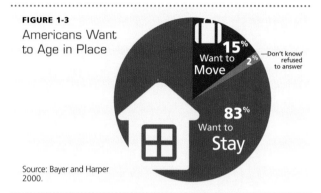

Source: Bayer and Harper
2000.

Another trend that favors compact development is the expected long-term rise in gasoline prices associated with *peak* oil production. Oil production will peak because of the natural propensity to extract the largest and most accessible—and hence the least costly—sources of oil first. As quantities from those sources diminish, production levels can be maintained only by extracting from less accessible and more costly sources. Eventually, production levels become too costly to maintain and overall production declines. This phenomenon has already occurred in the United States and Mexico. The question now is, "When will peaking occur on a global scale?"

Although the higher prices may encourage extraction from unconventional sources, such as liquefied coal, oil shale, and tar sands, oil from these sources is substantially more expensive than conventional oil (and worse from the standpoint of global-warming potential). No matter how you look at it, the price of oil is going up, and so too will the price of gasoline.

Because compact development affords a less vehicle-dependent lifestyle than does sprawl, Americans living in compact urban areas will be better able to weather the economic storm of rapidly rising gasoline prices. Moreover, to the degree that the United States transitions to compact development, the country as a whole will be less dependent on regions of the world that are unstable, hostile, or especially vulnerable to terrorist attacks.

High gasoline prices are already having an effect on housing values. In "Driven to the Brink: How the Gas Price Spike Popped the Housing Bubble and Devalued the Suburbs," Cortright (2008) documents how the spike in gas prices during 2007–2008 most affected housing values in outlying suburban neighborhoods. As measured by the change in housing prices between 2006 and 2007, distant suburbs saw the largest declines, whereas values in close-in neighborhoods held up better, and in some cases continued to increase. Those metropolitan areas with the strongest core neighborhoods saw the smallest declines in housing values at the metropolitan level.

Nelson (2006) projects that by 2025, the demand for attached and small-lot housing will exceed the current supply by 35 million units (71 percent), whereas the demand for large-lot housing will fall short of the current supply (see figure 1-5). If he is correct, the United States already has too much of the traditional suburban-style housing and too little dense, small-lot, pedestrian-oriented development.

FIGURE 1-4

Housing Price Declines Greatest at the
Suburban Fringe (2006 Q4 to 2007 Q4)

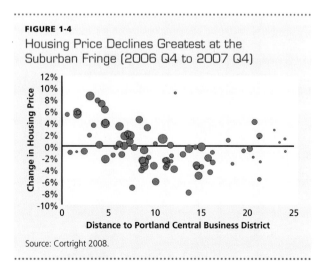

Source: Cortright 2008.

FIGURE 1-5

2003 Housing Supply versus 2025
Housing Demand

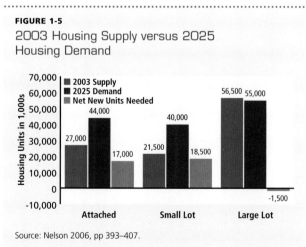

Source: Nelson 2006, pp 393–407.

The Market Begins to Respond

NEW FORMS OF DEVELOPMENT are beginning to address changing demands. Characterized by denser, more mixed-use development patterns that enable people to get around on foot and by transit, the new forms go by many names, including *walkable communities*, *new urbanism*, and *transit-oriented developments*. Infill and brownfield developments put unused parcels in urban and inner-suburban areas to new uses, taking advantage of existing infrastructure and nearby destinations. Single-use, automobile-focused shopping malls are being replaced with open-air shopping districts on connected streets with housing and office space above stores. And many communities have rediscovered and revitalized their traditional downtowns and town centers, often adding more housing to the mix. These varied development types are collectively referred to in this publication as *compact development* or *smart growth*.

These alternative models of land development tend to be the most desirable types in the market. *Emerging Trends in Real Estate*, an annual report by the Urban Land Institute and PricewaterhouseCoopers, notes in its 2011 edition, "Many stand-alone developments in car-dependent suburban areas have had problematic outcomes. ... Younger professionals want walkable centers where they don't have to get into a car to have lunch or do errands ..." (ULI and PWC 2010, p. 43). New urban and smart growth communities are in such high demand that they not only command a price premium at the point of purchase, but they also hold their premium values over time (Eppli and Tu 1999, 2007; Plaut and Boarnet 2003). The price premium can range from 40 to 100 percent compared with houses in nearby single-use subdivisions (Leinberger 2008). It is a matter of supply and demand. By all accounts, the demand for compact development is at least one-third of the new-home market, whereas the supply is a fraction of that.

It is commonly said that development practices change slowly. Bank lending practices, developer risk aversion, and simple human nature tend to keep today's new houses and commercial centers looking a lot like yesterday's. But there is evidence that things are changing much more rapidly than we might think. The new urbanist movement began in the 1980s. By 2003, 647 new urbanist developments were in some state of planning or construction (CNU 2003). Today, the Congress for the New Urbanism reports that so many new urbanist projects are under way that keeping track of them all is impossible. Similar trends can be observed in transit-oriented developments, with an estimated 117 having been constructed in ten years (Cervero 2003). Open-air shopping centers fashioned after main streets saw a 35 percent increase from 2000 to 2005 (Robaton 2005). Finally, the U.S.

Price premiums range from 9 to 13 percent for homes in new urbanist communities (Southern Village, North Carolina; Kentlands, Maryland). | *Southern Village; Adrienne Schmitz*

Green Building Council's rating and certification system for green development, Leadership in Energy and Environmental Design for Neighborhood Development (LEED-ND), attracted more than 230 applications from land developers, many more than expected by the program sponsors. As of January 2013, 113 pilot projects had achieved at least one stage of certification, and another 15 projects had been certified under LEED-ND 2009.

Resources and Appendixes

THE CHECKLISTS IN CHAPTERS 3 THROUGH 5 are the heart and soul of this manual. They draw primarily on six sources—the classic urban design literature, listed below, and materials listed in five appendixes:

- **A**—travel behavior studies linking features of the urban environment to walking and transit use;
- **B**—visual surveys identifying preferences for urban environmental features;
- **C**—hedonic price studies identifying features that add to the value of property;
- **D**—the traffic safety literature; and
- **E**—the best transit-oriented design manuals.

Appendixes A through E, described on the following page, are available at www.lib.utah.edu/pedtransit.

Classic Urban Design Literature

Classic readings in urban design and site planning are given due credit here. Readings that came early and shaped the thinking of those who followed include:

- Alexander, Christopher, Sara Ishikawa, and Murray Silverstein. 1977. *A Pattern Language: Towns, Buildings, Construction*. New York: Oxford University Press.
- Jacobs, Jane. 1961. *The Death and Life of Great American Cities*. New York: Random House.
- Lynch, Kevin. 1962. *Site Planning*. Cambridge, MA: MIT Press (latest edition coauthored with Gary Hack and published by MIT Press in 1984).
- Unwin, Raymond. 1909. *Town Planning in Practice*. London: T. Fisher Unwin Ltd. (reissued by Princeton Architectural Press, New York, 1994).

Seminal works in specialty areas of design include:

- Appleyard, Donald. 1981. *Livable Streets*. Berkeley: University of California Press.
- Arnold, Henry F. 1993. *Trees in Urban Design*. New York: Van Nostrand Reinhold.
- Gehl, Jan. 1987. *Life between Buildings*. New York: Van Nostrand Reinhold.
- Jacobs, Allan. 1993. *Great Streets*. Cambridge, MA: MIT Press.
- Trancik, Roger. 1986. *Finding Lost Space: Theories of Urban Design*. New York: Van Nostrand Reinhold.
- Untermann, Richard K. 1984. *Accommodating the Pedestrian: Adapting Towns and Neighborhoods for Walking and Bicycling*. New York: Van Nostrand Reinhold.
- Whyte, William H. 1980. *The Social Life of Small Urban Spaces*. Washington, DC: Conservation Foundation.
- Whyte, William H. 1988. *City: Rediscovering the Center*. New York: Doubleday.

There are also classic works on less critical subjects, such as signage, public art, street furniture, and parking lot design.

- Fleming, Robert Lee, and Renata von Tscharner. 1981. *Place Makers: Public Art That Tells You Where You Are*. Cambridge, MA: Townscape Institute.
- Gibbons, Johanna, and Bernard Oberholzer. 1992. *Urban Streetscapes: A Workbook for Designers*. New York: Van Nostrand Reinhold.
- McDonald, Shannon S. 2007. *The Parking Garage: Design and Evolution of a Modern Urban Form*. Washington, DC: Urban Land Institute.

Finally, a few books are so cleverly written and neatly packaged as to stand out from other broad-brush works. For local officials, planning students, or citizen activists, these may be the best places to start learning about urban design.

- Bacon, Edmund. 1974. *Design of Cities*. New York: Viking Press.
- Calthorpe, Peter. 1993. *The Next American Metropolis: Ecology, Community, and the American Dream*. New York: Princeton Architectural Press.
- Hedman, Richard. 1984. *Fundamentals of Urban Design*. Chicago: American Planning Association.
- Lynch, Kevin. 1960. *The Image of the City*. Cambridge, MA: Joint Center for Urban Studies.
- Sucher, David. 1995. *City Comforts: How to Build an Urban Village*. Seattle: City Comforts Press.

APPENDIX A:
Travel Behavior Studies

The potential to influence travel demand through changes in the built environment is the subject of more than 200 empirical studies. It has become the most heavily researched subject in urban planning. The best of the recent studies are summarized in appendix A. Elasticities of vehicle-miles traveled, walking, and transit use with respect to built environment variables are extracted from selected studies and combined in a meta-analysis. These composite elasticities are directly applicable to pedestrian- and transit-oriented design guidelines, as they tell us which variables have the most influence on walking and transit use.

APPENDIX B:
Visual Preference Surveys

Visual surveys show stakeholders a variety of images and ask them to rate or rank them with respect to walkability, sense of place, and other criteria. In visual assessment studies, the underlying features of an image that cause it to be rated high or low are subsequently determined through statistical analysis. Hundreds of such surveys have been conducted, and dozens have found their way into the published literature. Appendix B recaps the methods and results of relevant surveys, and identifies pedestrian- and transit-oriented features from three exemplary surveys: one of bus stops, a second of streetscapes, and a third of urban scenes more generally.

APPENDIX C:
Hedonic Price Studies

Hedonic price analysis is a method of estimating the demand for or price of goods and services that do not have traditional monetary value in the marketplace. An established body of research has used this approach to estimate the value that buyers in real estate markets place on seemingly intangible characteristics, such as urban design features. Appendix C summarizes the relevant literature, focusing on the effects of open and public spaces, mixed uses, and street networks.

APPENDIX D:
Traffic Safety Studies

Development patterns and roadway designs both have traffic safety impacts. Appendix D reviews these impacts and reaches conclusions that run counter to accepted transportation engineering theory. First, the traffic environments of dense urban areas appear to be safer than the lower-volume environments of the suburbs. Second, although dense urban areas typically contain less "forgiving" design treatments—such as narrow lanes, frequent intersections and driveway turnouts, and street trees and other obstacles situated close to the roadway—these treatments appear to *enhance* a roadway's safety performance when compared with more conventional roadway designs.

APPENDIX E:
Transit-Oriented Design Manuals

More than 50 transit-oriented design manuals are reviewed in appendix E. These manuals overlap somewhat with the classic urban design literature, but transit-oriented design is both more and less than urban design—more in the sense that additional topics are covered, less in the sense that design issues tend to be dealt with superficially. Transit-oriented features discussed in appendix E include land uses, roadway designs, site plans, and pedestrian amenities that complement transit services.

NOTE

1 The compact, walkable community was described identically in both surveys as follows: "Such communities have a town center that is surrounded by residential neighborhoods. The town center has small shops, restaurants, government buildings, churches, and public transit (bus, rail) stops. Residential neighborhoods are clustered around the town center, providing easy access to work and shopping. Each neighborhood has a variety of housing types (apartments, townhomes, single family homes) and houses are built on smaller lots and are closer to the street. Streets are designed to accommodate cars, pedestrians, and bicyclists. In residential areas streets are narrower, slower, and quieter with sidewalks, trees, and on-street parking. In commercial areas, sidewalks are wide and comfortable, streets are lined with trees, and parking lots are less conspicuous. The community includes a network of parks and trails for walking and biking. It also has a clearly defined boundary in order to preserve open space for parks, farmlands, and forests."

CHAPTER 2

Urban Design
QUALITIES

SINCE 2000, A NUMBER OF TOOLS FOR MEASURING THE QUALITY of the walking environment have emerged. Generically called *walking audit instruments*, these tools are now used by researchers, local governments, and community groups to measure physical features related to walkability, such as building setback, block length, and street and sidewalk width. The Robert Wood Johnson Foundation's Active Living Research website alone hosts 16 such instruments (activelivingresearch.org).

Yet individual physical features may not tell us much about the experience of walking down a particular street. Specifically, they may not capture people's overall perceptions of the street environment, perceptions that may have complex or subtle relationships to physical features. The urban design literature points to numerous perceptual qualities that may affect the walking experience. Other fields also contribute, including architecture, landscape architecture, park planning, environmental psychology, and the growing visual preference and visual assessment literature.

Perceptual or urban design qualities are linked to walking behavior through the conceptual framework shown in figure 2-1. Perceptions intervene (or mediate) between the physical features of the environment and walking behavior. Physical features influence the quality of the walking environment both directly and indirectly through the perceptions and sensitivities of individuals.

Urban design qualities are different from such qualities as sense of comfort, sense of safety, and level of interest that reflect how individuals react to a place—how they assess the conditions there, given their own attitudes and preferences. Perceptions may produce different reactions in different people. They can be assessed with a degree of objectivity by outside observers; individual reactions cannot.

A literature review yielded a list of 51 perceptual qualities of the urban environment. Of the 51, eight were selected for further study based on the importance assigned to them in the literature: (1) imageability, (2) enclosure, (3) human scale, (4) transparency, (5) complexity, (6) coherence, (7) legibility, and (8) linkage. Of the eight, the first five were successfully measured in a manner that met tests of validity and reliability.

Note: This chapter is taken from Ewing and Handy (2009).

The approach was to have a panel of experts link specific physical features to urban design quality ratings for a sample of street scenes that had been videotaped. The panel members helped define urban design qualities of streetscapes, rated different scenes with respect to those qualities, and submitted to interviews as they assigned their ratings to provide the research team with qualitative insights into the physical features that influenced their ratings.

The following sections explain the eight urban design qualities that were operationalized by the expert panel, providing the literature relevant to each quality and outlining the qualitative responses from panel members. Appendix F includes a list of panel members and their quantitative assessments. (The appendixes are available at www.lib.utah.edu/pedtransit).

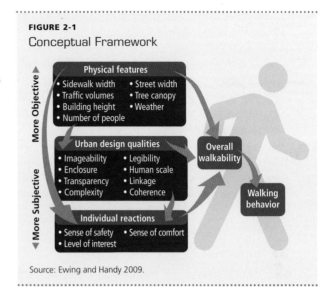

FIGURE 2-1
Conceptual Framework

More Objective → More Subjective

Physical features
- Sidewalk width
- Traffic volumes
- Building height
- Number of people
- Street width
- Tree canopy
- Weather

Urban design qualities
- Imageability
- Enclosure
- Transparency
- Complexity
- Legibility
- Human scale
- Linkage
- Coherence

Overall walkability

Walking behavior

Individual reactions
- Sense of safety
- Level of interest
- Sense of comfort

Source: Ewing and Handy 2009.

Imageability

IMAGEABILITY IS THE QUALITY OF A PLACE THAT MAKES IT DISTINCT, recognizable, and memorable. A place has high imageability when specific physical elements and their arrangement capture attention, evoke feelings, and create a lasting impression.

According to Kevin Lynch (1960), a highly imageable city is well formed, contains distinct parts, and is instantly recognizable to anyone who has visited or lived there. It plays to the innate human ability to see and remember patterns. It is a place whose elements are easily identifiable and grouped into an overall pattern.

Landmarks are a component of imageability. The term *landmark* does not necessarily denote a grandiose civic structure or even a large object. In Lynch's words, it can be "a doorknob or a dome." What is essential is its singularity and location, in relationship to its context and the city at large. Landmarks are a principle of urban design because they act as visual termination points, orientation points, and points of contrast in the urban setting. Tunnard and Pushkarev (1963, p. 140) attribute even greater importance to landmarks, saying, "A landmark lifts a considerable area around itself out of anonymity, giving it identity and visual structure."

Imageability is related to "sense of place." Gordon Cullen (1961, p. 152) elaborates on the concept of sense of place, asserting that a characteristic visual theme will contribute to a cohesive sense of place and will inspire people to enter and rest in the space. Jan

Imageability (Westwood Village, California).
| *Dan Burden*

Gehl (1987, p. 183) explains this phenomenon using the example of famous Italian city squares, where "life in the space, the climate, and the architectural quality support and complement each other to create an unforgettable total impression." When all factors manage to work together to such pleasing ends, a feeling of physical and psychological well-being results: the feeling that a space is a thoroughly pleasant place in which to be.

Imageability is influenced by many other urban design qualities—enclosure, human scale, transparency, complexity, coherence, legibility, and linkage—and is in some way the net effect of these qualities. Places that rate high on these qualities are likely to rate high on imageability as well—the neighborhoods of Paris or San Francisco, for example. However, places that rate low on these qualities may also evoke strong images, though ones that people may prefer to forget, such as boring industrial parks or strips of faceless shopping centers. Urban designers focus on the strength of positive images in discussing imageability and sense of place.

The urban design panel most often mentioned vernacular architecture as a contributor to imageability. Other influences mentioned were landmarks, striking views, unusual topography, and marquee signage.

Enclosure

ENCLOSURE REFERS TO THE DEGREE TO WHICH STREETS and other public spaces are visually defined by buildings, walls, trees, and other vertical elements. Spaces where the height of vertical elements is proportionally related to the width of the space between them have a room-like quality.

Outdoor spaces are defined and shaped by vertical elements, which interrupt viewers' lines of sight. A sense of enclosure results when lines of sight are so decisively blocked as to make outdoor spaces seem room-like. Cullen (1961, p. 29) states that "enclosure, or the out-door room, is, perhaps, the most powerful, the most obvious, of all the devices to instill a sense of position, of identity with the surroundings. … It embodies the idea of here-ness." Alexander, Ishikawa, and Silverstein (1977, p. 106) say that "an outdoor space is positive when it has a distinct and definite shape, as definite as the shape of a room, and when its shape is as important as the

Trees can help form a sense of enclosure (Madison, Wisconsin; Bethesda, Maryland). | *Dan Burden*

shapes of the buildings which surround it." In an urban setting, enclosure is formed by lining the street or plaza with unbroken building fronts of roughly equal height. The buildings become the "walls" of the outdoor room; the street and sidewalks become the "floor"; and if the buildings are roughly equal height, the sky projects as an invisible "ceiling." Buildings lined up that way are often referred to as *street walls*. Alexander, Ishikawa, and Silverstein (1977, pp. 489–91) state that the total width of the street, building to building, should not exceed the building heights in order to maintain a comfortable feeling of enclosure. Allan Jacobs (1993) is more lenient in this regard, suggesting that the proportion of building heights to street width should be at least 1:2. Other designers have recommended proportions as high as 3:2 and as low as 1:6.

At low suburban densities, building masses become less important in defining space, and street trees assume the dominant role. Rows of trees on both sides of a street can humanize the height-to-width ratio. Henry Arnold (1993) explains that trees define space both horizontally and vertically. Horizontally, they do so by visually enclosing or completing an area of open space. Vertically, they define space by creating an airy ceiling of branches and leaves. Unlike the solid enclosure of buildings, tree lines depend on visual suggestion and illusion. Street space will seem enclosed only if trees are closely spaced. Properly scaled, walls and fences can also provide spatial definition in urban and suburban settings.

Visual termination points may also contribute to a sense of enclosure. New urbanists such as Andrés Duany advocate closing vistas at street ends with prominent buildings, monuments, fountains, or other architectural elements as a way to achieve enclosure in all directions (Duany and Plater-Zyberk 1992). When the sides of a street are not strongly defined by buildings, focal points at its ends can maintain the visual linearity of the arrangement. Similarly, the layout of the street network can influence the sense of enclosure. A rectilinear grid with continuous streets creates long sight lines that may undermine the sense of enclosure created by the buildings and trees that line the street. Grids with nonorthogonal street connections, however, may create visual termination points that help enclose a space.

Enclosure is eroded by breaks in the continuity of the street wall, that is, breaks in the vertical elements, such as buildings or tree rows that line the street. Breaks in continuity that are occupied by nonactive uses create dead spaces that further erode enclosure; vacant lots, parking lots, driveways, and other uses that do not generate human activity and presence are all considered dead spaces. Large building setbacks are another source of dead space. Alexander, Ishikawa, and Silverstein (1977, p. 593) say, "Building setbacks from the street, originally invented to protect the public welfare by giving every building light and air, have actually helped greatly to destroy the street as social space."

The expert panel suggested that on-street parking, planted medians, and even traffic itself contribute to visual enclosure. They opined that the required building height to enclose street space varies with context, specifically, between a big city and a small town.

Human Scale

HUMAN SCALE REFERS TO A SIZE, TEXTURE, AND ARTICULATION of physical elements that match the size and proportions of humans and, equally important, correspond to the speed at which humans walk. Building details, pavement texture, street trees, and street furniture are all physical elements contributing to human scale.

The urban design glossary for the city of Seattle (2005, 2007) defines *human scale* as "the quality of a building that includes structural or architectural components of size and proportions that relate to the human form and/or that exhibits through its structural or architectural components the human functions contained within." Moderate-sized buildings, narrow streets, and small spaces create an intimate environment; the opposite is true for large buildings, wide streets, and open spaces.

What defines human scale is a matter of opinion. Experts set a range of three stories to six stories. For taller buildings, it has been suggested that lower floors should create a street wall but upper floors should step back before they ascend, giving human-scale definition to the street level but allowing for sunlight. Large buildings should make use of architectural detailing to help mitigate their large scale. For human scale, building widths should not be out of proportion with building heights, as are so many buildings in the suburbs. In

what was billed as the first of its kind, Stamps (1998) used a visual assessment survey to explore perceptions of architectural mass. The most important determinant was the cross-sectional area of buildings; second was the amount of window area; and third was the amount of facade articulation and partitioning.

Human scale can also be defined by human speed. Jane Holtz Kay (1997) argues that today, far too many things are built to accommodate the bulk and rapid speed of the automobile; we are "designing for 60 mph." When approached by foot, these things overwhelm the senses, creating disorientation. For example, large signs with large lettering are designed to be read by high-speed motorists. For pedestrians, small signs with small lettering that are perpendicular to the building facade are much more comfortable and more effective: large signs that are flush with the facade tend not to be visible by those passing by on the adjacent sidewalk.

Street trees can moderate the scale of tall buildings and wide streets. According to Henry Arnold (1993), where tall buildings or wide streets would intimidate pedestrians, a canopy of leaves and branches allows for a simultaneous experience of the smaller space within the larger volume. He posits that where streets are over 40 feet wide, additional rows of trees are needed to achieve human scale. Hedman (1984) recommends the use of other small-scale elements, such as clock towers, to moderate the scale of buildings and streets.

Jan Gehl (2010) demonstrates how distance plays a determinative role in personal interaction and hence designing for the human scale. At 300 to 500 meters (1,000–1,800 ft.), humans can identify other people as humans, instead of objects. From 25 to 100 meters (80–360 ft.), individual characteristics and body language can be observed. At less than 25 meters, people enter a "social" field of vision where "richness of detail and communication intensify dramatically meter by meter" (p. 35). Gehl then breaks the distances into four categories:

- Public distance: >12 feet
- Social distance: 4.5–12 feet
- Personal distance: 1.5–4.5 feet
- Intimate distance: 0–1.5 feet

According to Alexander, Ishikawa, and Silverstein (1977), a person's face is just recognizable at 70 feet, a loud voice can just be heard at 70 feet, and a person's face is recognizable in portrait-like detail up to about 48 feet. These distances set the limits of human scale for social interaction and, by extension, how space is designed. Gehl notes that the most highly regarded public squares in Europe are almost all smaller than 10,000 square meters (100,000 sq. ft.); most are smaller than 8,000 square meters.

In addition to the above elements, the expert panel related human scale to the intricacy of paving patterns, amount of street furniture, depth of setbacks on tall buildings, presence of parked cars, ornamentation of buildings, and spacing of windows and doors. Interestingly, high-rise Rockefeller Center and Times Square in New York City were both perceived as human scaled owing to compensating design elements at street level.

Transparency

TRANSPARENCY REFERS TO THE DEGREE TO WHICH PEOPLE CAN SEE or perceive what lies beyond the edge of a street or other public space and, more specifically, the degree to which people can see or perceive human activity beyond the edge of a street or other public space. Physical elements that influence transparency include walls, windows, doors, fences, landscaping, and openings into midblock spaces.

Taken literally, transparency is a material condition that is pervious to light or air, an inherent quality of substance as in a glass wall. A classic example of transparency is a shopping street with display windows that invite passersby to look in and then go in to shop. Blank walls and reflective glass buildings are classic examples of design elements that destroy transparency.

But transparency can be subtler than that. What lies behind the street edge need only be imagined, not actually seen. Allan Jacobs (1993) says that streets with many entryways contribute to the perception of human activity beyond the street, whereas those with blank walls and garages suggest that people are far away. Even blank walls may exhibit some transparency if overhung by trees or bushes, providing signs of habitation. Arnold (1993) tells us that trees with high canopies create "partially transparent tents," affording awareness of the space beyond while still conferring a sense of enclosure. By contrast, he notes that small trees in most urban settings work against transparency.

Transparency is most critical at the street level, because that is where the greatest interaction occurs between indoors and outdoors. Whyte (1988) suggests that if a blank wall index were ever computed as the percentage of blockfront up to a 35-foot height, it would show that blank walls have become the dominant feature of cityscapes. The ultimate in transparency is when internal activities are *externalized* or brought out to the sidewalk (Llewelyn-Davies 2000). Outdoor dining and outdoor merchandising are examples.

The expert panel suggested that courtyards, signs, and buildings that convey specific uses (for example, schools and churches) add to transparency. Reflective glass, arcades, and large building setbacks were thought to detract from transparency. Interior lighting was thought to increase the perception of transparency, whereas shadows were thought to decrease it.

Transparency (Charlotte, North Carolina; Seattle, Washington). | *Dan Burden; Eagle Rock Ventures LLC*

Complexity

COMPLEXITY REFERS TO THE VISUAL RICHNESS OF A PLACE. The complexity of a place depends on the variety of the physical environment, specifically the number and kinds of buildings, architectural diversity and ornamentation, landscape elements, street furniture, signage, and human activity.

Amos Rapoport (1990) explains the fundamental properties of complexity. Complexity is related to the number of noticeable differences to which a viewer is exposed per unit of time. People are most comfortable receiving information at perceivable rates. Too little information results in sensory deprivation; too much creates sensory overload. Similar to Kay's observations regarding human scale, Rapoport contrasts the complexity requirements of pedestrians and motorists. Slow-moving pedestrians require a high level of complexity to hold their interest, whereas fast-moving motorists will find the same environment chaotic. The suburban commercial strip is too complex and chaotic at driving speeds; yet because of its auto-oriented scale, it yields few noticeable differences at pedestrian speeds.

The environment can provide low levels of usable information in three ways: (1) elements may be too few or too similar; (2) elements, though numerous and varied, may be too predictable for surprise or novelty; or (3) elements, though numerous and varied, may be too unordered for comprehension. Pedestrians are apt to prefer streets high in complexity, since they provide interesting things to look at: building details, signs, people, sur-

faces, changing light patterns and movement, and signs of habitation. In *Life between Buildings*, Jan Gehl (1987, p. 143) notes that an interesting walking network will have the "psychological effect of making the walking distance seem shorter," by virtue of the trip being "divided naturally, into manageable stages." This effect helps explain why people will walk longer distances in urban settings than suburban ones.

Complexity results from varying building shapes, sizes, materials, colors, architecture, and ornamentation. According to Jacobs and Appleyard (1987), narrow buildings in varying arrangements add to complexity, whereas wide buildings subtract. Allan Jacobs (1993) refers to the need for many different surfaces over which light is constantly moving in order to keep eyes engaged. Tony Nelessen (1994, p. 224) asserts, "If a particular building or up to three buildings are merely repeated, the result will be boring and mass produced." Some variation can be incorporated into the building orientation plan or building setback line to allow for a varied building frontage instead of a monotonous, straight building facade. Too much setback variation, however, can undermine the sense of enclosure provided by a consistent street wall. Numerous doors and windows also produce complexity, as well as a degree of transparency.

Complexity is one perceptual quality that has been measured extensively in visual assessment studies. It has been related to changes in the textures, widths, heights, and setbacks of buildings (Elshestaway 1997), as well as to building shapes, articulation, and ornamentation (Heath, Smith, and Lim 2000; Stamps 1999).

Other elements of the built environment also contribute to complexity. According to Henry Arnold (1993), one function of trees is to restore the rich textural detail missing from modern architecture. Light filtered through trees gives life to space. Manipulation of light and shade

Complexity (Boulder, Colorado). |
Adrienne Schmitz

transforms stone, asphalt, and concrete into tapestries of sunlight and shadow. Street furniture also contributes to the complexity of street scenes. Allan Jacobs (1993) states that pedestrian-scaled streetlights, fountains, benches, special paving, and even public art combine to make regal, special places.

Signage is a major source of complexity in urban and suburban areas. If well done, signs can add visual interest, make public spaces more inviting, and help create a sense of place. Cullen (1961, p. 151) calls advertisement signs "the most characteristic, and, potentially, the most valuable, contribution of the twentieth century to urban scenery." When those signs are lit up at night, the result can be spectacular. However, signage must not be allowed to become chaotic and unfriendly to pedestrian traffic. Nasar (1987) reports that people prefer signage with moderate rather than high complexity—measured by the amount of variation among signs in location, shape, color, direction, and lettering style. Allan Jacobs (1993) uses Hong Kong signage as an example of complexity to the point of chaos.

The presence and activity of people add greatly to the complexity of a scene. They do so not only because people appear as discrete "objects" but because they are in constant motion. Gehl (1987, p. 25) explains that "people are attracted to other people. They gather with and move about with others and seek to place them-selves near others. New activities begin in the vicinity of events that are already in progress." In the course of his worldwide travels, Allan Jacobs (1993) found that the most popular streets were those that contained side-walks fairly cluttered with humans and life, calling them attractive obstacle courses that never failed to entertain.

Complexity can also arise at a larger scale from the pattern of development. Integration of land uses, housing types, activities, transportation modes, and people creates diversity, which in turn adds to complexity (Gehl 1987). Jane Jacobs (1961, p. 161) describes diversity as a mixture of commercial, residential, and civic uses in proximity to one another, creating human traffic throughout the day and night, and subsequently benefiting the safety, economic functioning, and appeal of a place.

The expert panel related complexity to
- layering of built elements at the edge of streets, from sidewalk to arcade to courtyard to building;
- diversity of building ages;
- diversity of social settings; and
- diversity of uses over the course of a day.

Two panel members lamented the loss of complexity as design becomes more controlled and predictable (as in some modern developments under unified ownership).

Coherence

COHERENCE REFERS TO A SENSE OF VISUAL ORDER. The degree of coherence is influenced by consistency and complementarity in the scale, character, and arrangement of buildings, landscaping, street furniture, paving materials, and other physical elements.

Allan Jacobs (1993, p. 287) describes coherence in architecture as follows: "Buildings on the best streets will get along with each other. They are not the same, but they express respect for one another, most particularly in respect to height and the way they look." According to Arnold (1993), complexity of architecture of earlier eras was given coherence by common materials, handcrafted details, and reflections of human use. When those elements are absent from architecture, landscaping becomes critical for creating a sense of visual unity; shade trees planted close together result in an uninterrupted pattern of light and shade, unifying a scene. At the city level, coherence takes the form of orderly density patterns and hierarchies of communal spaces (Alexander, Ishikawa, and Silverstein 1977). Nikos Salingaros (2000), applying mathematical principles to the urban setting, concludes, "Geometrical coherence is an identifiable quality that ties the city together through form, and is an essential prerequisite for the vitality of the urban fabric."

It is important to strike a balance between uniformity and idiosyncratic design. Hedman (1984, p. 29) warns that when every building seeks to be a unique statement and the center of attention, there is an unexpected effect: "Instead of providing an exciting counterpoint, the addition of each new and different building intensifies the impression of a nervous, irritating confusion." He lists multiple features of buildings

Coherence (Glendale, California).
| *Devon Meade & Ian Douglass*

that, when repeated, can create visual unity: building silhouettes, spacing between buildings, setbacks from street, proportions of windows/bays/doorways, massing of building form, location of entryways, surface material and finish, shadow patterns, building scale, style of architecture, and landscaping.

Although often presented as opposites, coherence and complexity represent distinct perceptual dimensions. Visual preference surveys show that viewers do not appreciate massive doses of unstructured information. People like complexity, but not the unstructured complexity of the commercial strip. Scenes with high complexity and low coherence tend to be least liked. In one such survey, Nasar (1987) found that people preferred signage that is moderately complex and highly coherent. Summarizing the results of many surveys, Kaplan and Kaplan (1989, p. 54) deem scenes of low complexity and high coherence as "boring," scenes of high complexity and low coherence as "messy," but scenes of high complexity and high coherence as "rich

and organized." It is important to note that coherence does not imply mindless repetition or blandness, rather continuity of design and thematic ordering.

The expert panel described coherence in relation to repeated elements: common building masses, building setbacks, street furniture, and landscaping. They emphasized that there could be ordered diversity and that without diversity, coherent design becomes monotonous.

Legibility

LEGIBILITY REFERS TO THE EASE WITH WHICH THE SPATIAL STRUCTURE of a place can be understood and navigated as a whole. The legibility of a place is improved by a street or pedestrian network that provides travelers with a sense of orientation and relative location and by physical elements that serve as reference points.

As described by Kevin Lynch (1960, p. 3) in his classic, *The Image of the City*, legibility is the apparent clarity of the cityscape, the "ease by which its parts can be recognized and can be organized into a coherent pattern." Lynch suggests that when faced with a new place, people automatically create a mental map that divides the city into paths, edges, districts, nodes, and landmarks. Places with strong edges, distinct landmarks, and busy nodes allow people to form detailed and relatively accurate mental maps. Conversely, a city that has no definite edges, nodes, or visually interesting features will be difficult to make sense of and to remember. Legibility facilitates wayfinding—the process by which people move successfully through the physical environment to reach a desired destination—which includes determining a route between two points, choosing an alternate route when the primary route is impassable, navigating along a route, and learning a new spatial environment.

The layout of the street network has an important influence on legibility, although the influence is sometimes ambiguous. A regular grid of streets makes it easy for people to navigate even when they are unfamiliar with a place, but it does not provide a way of distinguishing one block from another. An irregular pattern of streets, in which blocks are of irregular length and compass orientation changes from block to block, may increase the difficulty of navigating and learning the network, but it distinguishes each block with different lengths and orientations. The street network thus works together with other elements of the physical environment to determine the legibility of a place. Signage, in particular, helps distinguish one point from another and to orient and direct a traveler through the network. Landmarks, which have an important influence on imageability, also play an important role in mental maps and thus help increase the legibility of a place.

Visual termination and deflection points also contribute to legibility. Visual termination creates a focal point. New urbanists Andrés Duany and Elizabeth Plater-Zyberk (1992) say that visual terminations focus the community, as well as provide a degree of enclosure. On a large scale, visual termination points can include large civic buildings, prominent landmarks, or elements of nature. On a smaller, neighborhood scale, visual termination can be created by using small-scale elements, such as gazebos, landscaped traffic circles, or bends in the roads. Allan Jacobs (1993, p. 297) says of streets, "Since they have to start and stop somewhere, these points should be well marked." He argues that clearly marked end points both serve as reference points and give a sense of definition to an area.

Individual members of the expert panel defined legibility differently, some positing that legibility had more to do with the context of a street than the design of the street itself, and others positing the opposite.

Legibility (San Francisco, California). | *Dan Burden*

Linkage

LINKAGE REFERS TO PHYSICAL AND VISUAL CONNECTIONS—from building to street, building to building, space to space, or one side of the street to the other—that tend to unify disparate elements. Tree lines, building projections, and marked crossings all create linkage. Linkage can occur longitudinally along a street or laterally across a street.

Linkages can be defined as features that promote the interconnectedness of different places and that provide convenient access between them. Linkage is closely associated with the concept of connectivity, as both are concerned with the ease of movement in an area and depend on the relationships between paths and nodes. Allan Jacobs (1993) recommends urban intersections every 300 feet or fewer. Alexander, Ishikawa, and Silverstein (1977) give similar advice, suggesting pedestrian road crossings every 200 or 300 feet. They advocate the use of a separate pedestrian-only network running orthogonally to the street grid to maximize pedestrian accessibility. Duany and Plater-Zyberk (1992) generally limit the size of blocks to 230 by 600 feet to ensure reasonable travel distances. On the other hand, Appleyard (1981) argues against too much connectivity through residential areas since through-traffic can erode a sense of community; he suggests breaking up the gridiron with barriers and diverters that impede vehicles but allow for bicycle and pedestrian movement.

Linkages between the street and surrounding buildings are also important and may be psychological as well as physical. Maintenance of sight lines and sidewalk connections are obvious ways to provide this kind of linkage, but it can also be provided in more subtle ways. For example, Arnold (1993) advocates the use of trees for linkage: continuous tree rows can psychologically connect places at either end, and tree patterns that reflect or amplify building geometry can psychologically link buildings to the street. As Trancik (1986, p. 106) puts it, "Urban design is concerned with the question of making comprehensible links between discrete things."

As with legibility, members of the expert panel had difficulty defining linkage and had low interrater reliability in their ratings of street scenes. Linkage was mostly defined by the connectedness of things, and a grid street network was most often used to exemplify the quality of linkage.

Linkage (Boca Raton, Florida). | *Reid Ewing*

Conclusion

THE PRECEDING SECTIONS HAVE INTRODUCED EIGHT URBAN DESIGN QUALITIES, along with summaries of the literature behind each quality. These qualities are further illustrated in the checklists and more detailed descriptions in chapters 3 through 5. By considering these qualities, developers, planners, and policy makers can better understand the relationship between physical features of the street environment and walking behavior and, as a result, they can develop more effective urban design solutions for creating high-quality pedestrian environments.

CHAPTER 3

CHECKLIST
of Essential Features

- Medium-to-high densities
- Fine-grained mix of land uses
- Short- to medium-length blocks
- Transit routes every half mile or closer
- Two- to four-lane streets (with rare exceptions)

- Continuous sidewalks appropriately scaled
- Safe crossings
- Appropriate buffering from traffic
- Street-oriented buildings
- Comfortable and safe places to wait

Chapters 3, 4, and 5 present the checklists of design features that form the core of this book. The features are divided into three categories: essential, highly desirable, and worthwhile but not essential. This chapter presents the first checklist: the most essential elements.

Medium-to-High Densities

DEVELOPMENT DENSITIES IN THE UNITED STATES HAVE DECLINED DRAMATICALLY since the mid-20th century. Before mechanized transportation, gross densities were in the range of 40 to 80 people per acre; such densities compressed enough activities into a small area to allow people to walk to almost everything they needed. In the streetcar era, densities around transit stops were perhaps half as high. Today, in newly developing areas, gross densities are one-tenth the historical norm. Such low densities are practical only because the automobile allows people to overcome great distances at high speeds.

Every shred of available evidence points to the significance of density in promoting walking and transit use. Higher densities mean more residents or employees within walking distance of transit stops or stations. They mean more street life and the added interest and security that go with having more people around and more eyes on the street. They mean higher parking charges and more congestion for motorists, and they make possible lower auto ownership rates, and thus a greater propensity to walk or use transit.

Since the turn of the century, survey research shows an increasing amount of support for aspects of compact development, and some are now linking density to innovation and economic creativity (Knudsen et al. 2009). But the mere mention of higher densities still sends shivers down the spines of many residents and local officials. In this regard, density has gotten a bum rap. People often confuse density with crowding, *density* being the number of dwelling units per unit area and *crowding* the number of persons per room in dwelling units. Crowded conditions have no redeeming value, whereas high-density living can be very desirable, as evidenced by the high housing prices and rents commanded by such dense neighborhoods as Washington, D.C.'s Georgetown and Boston's Beacon Hill. Homebuyers are willing to pay a premium to locate in new urbanist developments that are typically denser than their conventional suburban counterparts. Compact developments can command price premiums of as much as 40 to 100 percent com-

pared with houses in nearby single-use subdivisions (Leinberger 2008).

People also confuse high density with high-rise buildings that tower over the surrounding neighborhood. Except in extremely dense developments, obtaining higher densities does not require the use of high rises. High densities can, in fact, be achieved through the use of small-scale structures by increasing the percentage of buildings that cover each lot. Lot coverages of 60, 70, or even 80 percent are common in the densest urban areas (Belmont 2002).

The key difference is in the treatment of vehicle parking. High-coverage buildings almost universally accommodate parking in multilevel structures (aboveground or underground). Conversely, and somewhat ironically, many high-rise buildings are surrounded by vast

LOCAL CODE EXAMPLES

Density

Both of the following codes promote higher densities around transit stations as part of transit-oriented development policies. In Aurora, Colorado, the zoning code sets a range of minimum densities that decrease with distance from the transit station. Interestingly, Aurora does not set a maximum density in the core area that immediately surrounds the transit station. San Diego requires an average density rather than a minimum density. Although San Diego's average density requirement of 18 units per acre is much lower than Aurora's, it appears sufficient to support transit and to provide an active street life. San Diego offers an incentive for density in the form of a density bonus for projects planned in proximity to existing or planned transit stations.

AURORA, COLORADO | BUILDING AND ZONING CODE

Transit-Oriented District

PRINCIPLE. Residential densities in TODs are higher than in surrounding areas, and usually transition from higher densities near the transit station to lower densities adjacent to surrounding neighborhoods. Higher densities provide increased numbers of transit riders within walking distance of rail stations and provide for lively, interesting places. There shall be no upper limit for residential densities in the core sub-area and those densities shall generally exceed 60 units per acres.

2. REQUIRED DENSITIES. Residential densities shall be determined by the station area plan. Where no station area plan has been adopted, minimum densities shall be as follows:

- **CORE AREA:** 60 units per acre
- **GENERAL AREA:** 40 units per acre
- **TRANSITION AREA:** 20 units per acre

Aurora, Colo., Building and Zoning Code ch. 146, art. 7, div. 6, § 146-728(C) (2009).

SAN DIEGO, CALIFORNIA | MUNICIPAL CODE

Urban Village Overlay Zone

DENSITY. The combined mixed-use core and residential components of the urban village shall have an average density of at least 18 dwelling units per net acre. Maximum permitted density shall be determined by the base zone regulations. A 10 percent density bonus over the base zone density may be permitted for projects located within 2,000 feet of an existing or planned light rail transit station or other trunk transit line station, unless stated otherwise in the applicable land use plan.

San Diego, Cal., Mun. Code ch. 13, art. 2, div. 11, § 132.1107(a) (2009).

LEFT: **At Addison Circle, in Addison, Texas, low-rise, high-coverage buildings create density in a pedestrian-oriented neighborhood;** BELOW: **Low density at the ground level discourages pedestrian activity (San Francisco, Califonia).**
| *RTKL; Wilson Meany Sullivan*

expanses of surface parking lots and, as such, achieve only moderate levels of density. In the exceptionally useful volume *Visualizing Density* (Campoli and MacLean 2007), examples illustrate that equally high densities can be achieved with low-rise, high-coverage buildings as with high-rise, low-coverage buildings.

Pedestrians are uncomfortable with high-rise towers, low lot coverages, and especially large parking lots. They are more comfortable with small-scale buildings and high lot coverages, which provide the important urban design qualities of enclosure, human scale, and complexity (see chapter 2). Indeed, "much of the criticism of high-rise living and its socially alienating effects is not due to its high density but to its low density at ground level," where nearly all human interaction must occur (Newman and Hogan 1981, pp. 269–303). The modernist ideal, articulated by Le Corbusier, of high-rise "buildings in a park" has in many cases been experienced in practice as "buildings in a parking lot" (Kunstler 1993, p. 79).

FIGURE 3-1
Bethesda Central Business District Plan

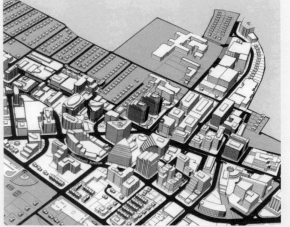

Source: Montgomery County, Maryland, Planning Department.

High-density mixed use within 1,500 feet of a Metrorail station (Bethesda, Maryland). | *Cooper Carry*

How dense is dense enough? For the purpose of supporting cost-effective transit service, transit-oriented design (TOD) manuals attempt to establish minimum density thresholds that will, on average, generate sufficient ridership to justify different levels of transit service. The standards articulated in these manuals, however, stretch between two and 40 residential units per acre, an unwieldy range with surprisingly little empirical foundation. We must thus look elsewhere for numerical guidance.

In Miami, an overall average density of 23 residents or employees per acre is required to support basic bus service (Messenger and Ewing 1996). This figure translates into 8.4 dwelling units per acre, slightly higher than the long-accepted minimum transit service standard of seven units per acre set by Pushkarev and Zupan (1977). In areas of the city receiving premium bus service, residential densities rise to more than 11 units per acre. These density levels generally occur within the first quarter mile of the city's transit stops, tapering off as the distance from the stops increases. Because transit ridership rates tend to drop dramatically beyond the first quarter mile surrounding a transit stop, the colocation

The distinction between high-rise and high-coverage buildings illustrates some of the differences between perceived density and measured density, two qualities that are often confused. We know, for example, that densities are perceived to be lower where there is open green space nearby, where blocks are short, where buildings are of moderate height, and in the case of high-rise buildings, where the ground floor comprises direct-entry residences (MacDonald 2005). People also tend to accept higher densities in transit-oriented development in exchange for easy access to rail and the availability of amenities, in particular open space and retail services (Cervero and Bosselmann 1998).

FIGURE 3-2

Net Density Requirements for Urban Livability

Author	Units/Acre
Jane Jacobs	100
Steve Belmont	25–100
Kevin Lynch	12–20
Allan Jacobs and Donald Appleyard	15
Peter Calthorpe	10–15

Sources: Belmont 2002, pp. 204–7; Calthorpe 1993, p. 83; A. Jacobs and Appleyard 1987, pp. 112–20; J. Jacobs 1961, pp. 208–12; Lynch 1960, pp. 146–47.

FIGURE 3-3

Transit Density Thresholds

TOD Typology	Minimum Housing Density (units/acre)	Housing Type	Example
Urban downtown	>60	Multifamily	Printers Row (Chicago, Illinois)
Urban neighborhood	>20	Multifamily, townhouse, single family	Mockingbird Station (Dallas, Texas) Barrio Logan (San Diego, California)
Suburban center	>50	Multifamily, townhouse	Clarendon Market Commons (Arlington, Virginia)
Suburban neighborhood	>12	Multifamily, townhouse, single family	The Crossings (Mountain View, California)
Commuter town center	>12	Multifamily, townhouse, single family	Prairie Crossing (Grayslake, Illinois)

Source: Dittmar and Ohland 2004, p. 37.

of Miami's density gradients and transit corridors creates an optimal transit-density geographic pattern.

These density levels, however, support only a minimum to moderate level of transit service, and they assume a fairly low level of transit ridership productivity. They represent, in fact, that point at which auto dependence just begins to give way to multimodalism. For moderate to high transit ridership levels, frequent transit service, active street life, and viable neighborhood businesses, higher densities are required (see figures 3-2 and 3-3). The area surrounding the Bethesda, Maryland, Metrorail station, for example, has a gross density of 33 units per acre, and a pronounced step-down density pattern with distance from the station (see figure 3-1). An impressive 36 percent of resident commutes are by transit, and 15 percent are by walking.

Fine-Grained Mix of Land Uses

SINCE THE RISE OF THE AUTOMOBILE, urban activities have become increasingly compartmentalized. Places where most Americans work, shop, learn, and play are remote from one another, and none is within walking distance of home, leaving the automobile as the only convenient way to get to such places. So-called clean zoning has further enshrined the problem by designating large areas for single uses only.

From empirical studies, we know that a diverse land-use mix has a stronger influence on rates of both walking and transit use than does density. In a study specifically of mixed-use developments (MXDs), Ewing et al. (2011) find that external vehicle trips (those from the MXD to outside destinations) decline substantially as the numbers of jobs and residents within the MXD become more balanced. The share of walking trips to external destinations increases substantially as the number of jobs within a mile increases. This effect occurs for several reasons. A blend of nonresidential and residential uses places trip origins and destinations within walking distance of each other; people are much more likely to walk when they have some place specific and nearby to go. *Residential accessibility*—the proximity of out-of-home activities to one's place of residence—affects the length, mode, and arguably even the frequency of home-based trips. Over the course of a typical day, the level of residential accessibility determines a person's spatial footprint—that is, the amount of geographic space traversed to accomplish the day's basic tasks (Fan and Khattak 2008)—which, of course, determines the amount and type of travel undertaken.

A second type of accessibility gets less attention but is also important. *Destination accessibility*—the proximity of out-of-home activities to one another—affects

A single-use downtown is active at lunchtime but dead after hours (Des Moines, Iowa). | *Reid Ewing*

Residential and destination accessibility (Washington, D.C.). | © Eric Taylor

the ability of travelers to link trips efficiently into tours or, better still, to complete multiple activities at a single stop. In nonresidential areas, a mix of uses allows people to run errands on the way to and from work, and at lunchtime. Transit users can run errands on the way to and from stops (much as auto users run errands on the way to and from their primary destinations). A study of street life in Boston found that the liveliest blocks have seven to eight businesses for every 200 feet (Mehta 2009, p. 60).

Other pedestrian-oriented qualities often ascribed to mixed-use development include architectural variety and visual interest, street security due to continual *eyes on the street*, and a greater sense of community when residents have places outside home and work to casually interact. The perceptual quality of complexity is also frequently enhanced by the mixing of land uses (see chapter 2).

Mixed use can be defined by the distance people are willing to walk. With the median walking distance in the United States hovering around one-quarter mile, that would seem to be the outer limit on the scale at which uses can still be considered mixed (Agrawal and Schimek 2007). Shorter distances and finer mixes are clearly better.

Jane Jacobs (1961) distinguishes between mixed primary uses—for example, residential, employment, and service—and mixed secondary uses, such as shops, restaurants, pubs, and other small-scale facilities. The objective, for Jacobs, is to achieve a mix at both levels so

Horizontal and vertical mixed use (Arlington, Virginia; San Jose, California). | © Eric Taylor; Adrienne Schmitz

that the ebb and flow of people over a given streetscape occur at many different times during the course of the day. The Urban Land Institute's definition of *mixed use* emphasizes the functional and physical integration of at least three significant land uses (Schwanke et al. 2003). The aforementioned study by Ewing et al. (2011, p. 251) modifies the ULI definition in this way: "A mixed-use development or district consists of two or more land uses between which trips can be made using local streets, without having to use major streets. The uses may include residential, retail, office, and/or entertainment. There may be walk trips between the uses."

Rowley (1996) presents a highly nuanced conceptual model of mixed use that combines grain (the amount of space between uses), scale (buildings, blocks, streets, and districts), density (which is inextricably bound up with mixed use), and permeability (the degree of pedestrian pathways through the space). Hoppenbrouwer and Louw (2005) build on Rowley's model, adding several

FIGURE 3-4

Three Views of the Ideal Land Use Mix

Source	Land Use	Percent of Mix
Alexander, Ishikawa, and Silverstein	Housing	26
	Shops and restaurants	7
	Community functions	15
	Hotels	5
	Offices	16
	Manufacturing	12
	Parking	19
Calthorpe	Housing	20–60
	Commercial	30–70
	Public uses	5–15
Ewing	Housing	41
	Commercial	10
	Civic	12
	Recreation/open space	15
	Rights-of-way	22

Sources: Alexander, Ishikawa, and Silverstein 1977, p. 34; Calthorpe 1993, p. 63; Ewing 1996, p. 21.

LOCAL CODE EXAMPLES

Mixed Use

In encouraging a mixture of land uses, the code of St. Lucie County, in Florida, takes a citywide approach, requiring a mix of uses in each neighborhood. Rather than simply allowing different types of uses, St. Lucie's code requires that each neighborhood contain a minimum number of retail and civic building lots. St. Lucie provides for continuous street walls and accounts for transitions in scale and type, placing considerable emphasis on urban design and aesthetic impact. Portland, Oregon's code creatively uses traditional zones and overlay zones to provide for a mixture of uses. Portland's neighborhood commercial zone contains flexibility to foster different uses, and it limits the size of commercial uses so as to moderate potential negative consequences of mixing residential and commercial uses.

ST. LUCIE COUNTY, FLORIDA

Land Development Regulations

Each neighborhood must contain a mixture of lot types to provide a variety of uses and diverse housing options within the neighborhood. Differing lot types may be placed back-to-back on a single block to provide harmonious transitions between lot types. Lot types should be selected to provide buildings of like scale and massing on opposite sides of streets. Each neighborhood must contain at least one Mixed-Use or Retail Building Lot. Each neighborhood must contain at least three Civic Building Lots; one civic building must be constructed within two years after development commences.

St. Lucie County, Fla., Land Dev. Code ch. 3, § 3.01.03.EE.2.e(1) (2009).

PORTLAND, OREGON | ZONING CODE

Neighborhood Commercial Base Zone

The zone encourages the provision of small-scale retail and service uses for nearby residential areas. Some uses which are not retail or service in nature are also allowed so a variety of uses may locate in existing buildings. Uses are restricted in size to promote a local orientation and to limit adverse impacts on nearby residential areas. Development is intended to be pedestrian oriented and compatible with the scale of surrounding residential areas. Parking areas are restricted, since their appearance is generally out of character with the surrounding residential development and the desired orientation of the uses.

Portland, Ore., Zoning Code § 33.130.030(A) (2009).

FIGURE 3-5

Activities Linked to Work and Shopping Trips (Palm Beach County, Florida)

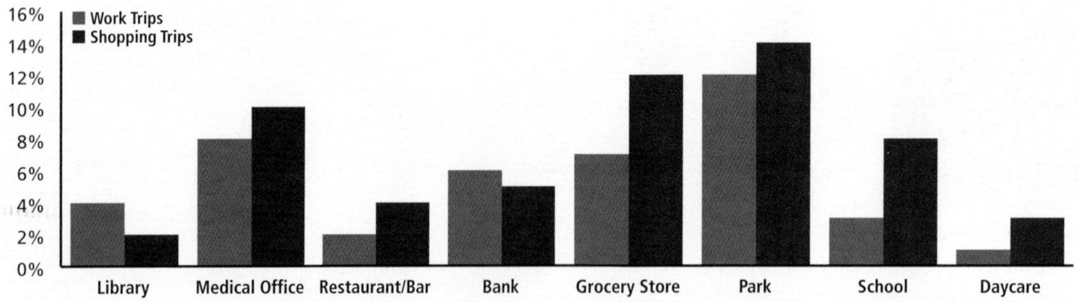

Source: Ewing 1996, p.26.

dimensions, including aspect (horizontal versus vertical use mixing), shared premises (different uses in the same space), and time (different uses over the course of a day, week, or year). Their resulting typology reduces the concept of mixed use to just four definitional features: functions, dimensions, scale, and texture.

A few intrepid souls have attempted to define the ideal mix of land uses. Their views are summarized in figure 3-4. Perhaps more defensible empirically are the results of household travel surveys, which tell us which activities tend to be combined with work and shopping in multipurpose trips and tours. Figure 3-5, based on a household travel survey in Palm Beach County, Florida, shows which land uses are so linked and hence belong within employment and shopping centers, and around transit stops and stations.

Short- to Medium-Length Blocks

SINCE THE MID-20TH CENTURY, THERE HAS BEEN A TREND TOWARD LARGER BLOCKS and, correspondingly, fewer street intersections. This trend is true not only in the suburbs, where superblocks are the norm, but also in central cities where blocks plus interior rights-of-way have been consolidated to create larger building sites. In cities like Detroit where the impacts of postwar urban renewal are particularly evident, the creation of superblocks has reduced block frontage (the sum of all streetside edges of all blocks in a particular area) by more than 35 percent (B. Ryan 2008). This practice of block consolidation "contributes to a city scaled to cars and is a grave error," assuming pedestrian-friendliness is the goal (Sucher 1995, p. 131).

Block size has been shown to be as strongly related to walking and transit use as the previous two essential features, density and mixed land uses. In fact, in some studies, the effect of block size appears to be even stronger (Cervero 1994).

The increased walkability that smaller blocks provide also appears to be valued in real estate markets. A hedonic price study of homes in Portland, Oregon, for example, finds that homebuyers are willing to pay a premium for houses in neighborhoods with connective street networks and better pedestrian accessibility to commercial uses. Although a number of factors lead to increased prices, the study concludes that "much of the premium comes from improvements in internal connectivity that stem from smaller blocks, and shorter streets" (Song and Knaap 2003, p. 236).

The reasons why walkability depends on block size are numerous. Most obviously, having more intersections means having more places where cars must stop and pedestrians can cross. Also, short blocks and frequent cross streets create the potential for more direct routing; that is important to pedestrians, much more so than to high-speed motorists. Finally, a dense network of streets disperses traffic so that each street carries less traffic

Long suburban and short urban blocks (Cedar Falls, Iowa; Washington, D.C.).
| *Dan Burden; District of Columbia Office of Planning*

and can be scaled accordingly, making streets more pleasant to walk along and easier to cross (Charlotte Department of Transportation 2007, pp. 62–63).

There may be optical and psychological factors at work as well. The maximum distance at which the human eye can perceive a detail that is one centimeter in size is approximately 150 feet; beyond that distance, human visual acuity degrades rapidly (Geisler and Albrecht 2000, pp. 85–86). Hence, as intersection frequencies increase and approach that 150-foot standard, the percentage of time that a moving pedestrian spends within the fine-detail focal distance of the next intersection also increases. It has been suggested that more frequent intersections give pedestrians a greater sense of freedom and control, as they need not always take the same path to a given destination. It also makes the walk seem more eventful, and the space more porous and public, since it is punctuated by frequent crossing of streets (Thibaud 2001). Finally, more intersections may

shorten the sense of elapsed time on walking trips, since progress is judged to some extent against the milestone of reaching the next intersection (Sucher 1995, p. 131).

By mapping different cities at a common scale, Allan Jacobs (1993, pp. 260–62) determined that Venice, Italy, has about 1,500 intersections in a typical square mile, whereas the city of Irvine, outside Los Angeles, California, has 15 intersections per square

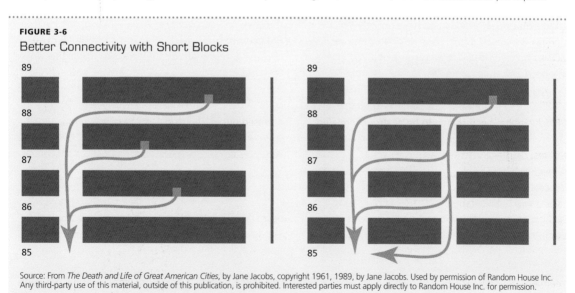

FIGURE 3-6
Better Connectivity with Short Blocks

FIGURE 3-7
Street Maps at the Same Scale for Venice, Italy, Los Angeles, and Irvine, California

Source: A. Jacobs, 1993, p. 221.

mile. Downtown Los Angeles has about one-tenth as many intersections as Venice, and ten times as many as Irvine. People familiar with those three cities would doubtlessly rank their walkability in the same order. Allan Jacobs also found that downtown Boston had, at the time of his writing, lost more than one-third of its historic intersections. Salt Lake City, like many western U.S. cities, is noted for its large block sizes (ten acres per block). In studying how to improve walkability, the city planning department compared Salt Lake's blocks with those of other North American cities, finding that four Salt Lake blocks cover the same territory as 36 Portland, Oregon, blocks. To overcome the negative effects that these large blocks have on walking, the city has developed a plan for breaking up the blocks, at least for pedestrians, by inserting midblock pass-throughs and street crossings.

These measures seem to comport with current directions in the urban form of city centers. In his analysis of cities in Australia, Canada, and the United States, Siksna (1997, 1998) finds that since the 1960s, with the end of the post–World War II urban renewal era, cities with small- to medium-sized blocks (five acres or less) have tended to keep their blocks intact (that is, they have not combined them into superblocks), whereas cities with large blocks (more than five acres) have tended over time to break up their blocks with alleys and streets. The primary reason for this transformation is the congruency of smaller blocks to the lotting patterns, building forms, and street frontage requirements favored by today's central-city real estate markets. In a *Back to the Future* way, this shift is, to a certain degree, following historic precedent: when laying out Portland, Oregon's initial street system in 1845, the original incorporators chose the city's now legendary 200- by 200-foot block pattern, not because it is pedestrian friendly (which it is), but because corner properties sell and rent for higher prices, and having smaller blocks meant having more corners (Lansing 2003). This configuration is ideal for small-scale commerce (J. Jacobs 1961, pp. 179–81).

Maximum block lengths are sometimes regulated in land development codes, with standards that vary from

FIGURE 3-8
Block Length Guidelines for Charlotte, North Carolina

Street Type	Block Length	Notes
Main street	400 feet maximum	
Avenue	600 feet maximum	Median cuts may occur every 600 feet.
Boulevard	1,000–1,200 feet typical between signalized intersections, median cuts, or left-overs	Side streets should be more closely spaced.
Parkway	½ mile minimum	Shorter blocks are allowable only when existing intermediate streets cannot be closed or land parcel configuration makes them necessary.

Source: Charlotte Department of Transportation 2007, chap. 4.

Midblock pass-through (Charleston, South Carolina). | *Dan Burden*

200 to 1,500 feet (Handy, Paterson, and Butler 2003). In some ordinances, such as Charlotte, North Carolina's, the standards vary with the functional type of street bordering the block (see figure 3-8). This control is a form of access management, used mainly to maintain through-capacity on the highest-order streets. As through-streets get closer together, intersection density and street capacity both increase, supporting the additional traffic that usually accompanies higher densities (Ewing 2000b).

If blocks are more than 600 to 800 feet on a side, they are, functionally, scaled to the automobile and midblock crosswalks and pass-throughs are recommended (S. Smith et al. 1987, p. 25). Many of the long east–west blocks in New York and north–south blocks in Charleston, South Carolina, have such features. Alleys serve the same purpose. Although these interventions are important for mitigating the negative effects of oversized blocks, they are poor substitutes for the real thing: frequent intersections connected to active streets.

LOCAL CODE EXAMPLES ## Block Lengths

Madison, Wisconsin's zoning code takes a very simple approach to restricting block length, providing a general limitation of 500 feet and permitting limited exceptions. The exception for topography provides flexibility in recognition of local conditions. By requiring approval for exceptions, the code provides some safeguard against overuse of the exceptions process. Albuquerque's approach is slightly more complex. Albuquerque's code requires considerably smaller blocks, limiting block size to 400 feet and requiring that blocks over 300 feet provide midblock pedestrian access. Albuquerque also provides for some flexibility in recognition of existing conditions, but includes provisions requiring that midblock access points be provided during redevelopment in areas where block size exceeds 400 feet.

MADISON, WISCONSIN
Zoning Code

In the R2S District, block lengths shall not, as a general rule, exceed 500 feet in length between street lines, unless required by exceptional topography or other limiting factors when approved by the Plan Commission.

Madison, Wis., Code § 28.08(13)(i) (2009).

ALBUQUERQUE, NEW MEXICO
Form-Based Code

BLOCK SIZE. Block perimeter for new development shall not exceed a maximum of 1600 feet. No block shall exceed 400 feet in length measured from center of R.O.W. [Right of Way]. Block lengths longer than 300 feet shall be provided with mid-block access points. If a block size in a developed area exceeds these standards, mid-block pedestrian access points shall be included in any redevelopment projects such that block lengths do not exceed 400 feet. The Planning Director may modify block size standards based on limitations of existing conditions.

Albuquerque, N.M., Code § 14-16-3-22(B)(1)(i)(1) (2009).

High service coverage (San Francisco, California). | *Dan Burden*

Transit Routes Every Half Mile or Closer

AS CITY BLOCKS HAVE BEEN REPLACED BY SUPERBLOCKS, the distance between through-streets has increased. Within these large blocks, straight, continuous streets have given way to curving, discontinuous streets. The combination of curvilinear local streets and widely spaced through-streets has left fewer people within walking distance of transit lines (see figure 3-9).

In choosing whether or not to take transit, potential riders are substantially influenced by the distance from, and amount of time it will take them to walk to, the transit stop. That calculation is further influenced by characteristics of the potential rider, the station area and neighborhood, transit stop and route features, and climate (Murray and Wu 2003; Zhao et al. 2003). Transit use drops by 0.14 percent for every 1 percent increase in distance to the nearest transit stop. Typically, TOD manuals assume walking distances from one-eighth to one-half mile, and the old transit industry standard—that transit users will walk a quarter mile, or five minutes at three miles per hour, to a bus stop—is still fairly realistic.

LOCAL CODE

EXAMPLES

Transit Routes

Aurora, Colorado's street standards emphasize coordinating with the regional transit authority, calling for bus routes every half mile and intersection designs that accommodate buses. San Diego's code contains general language calling for locating transit stops to "maximize access" and optimize pedestrian and cycling connectivity. The code provides more specificity in the context of major activity zones, stating that stops should be every quarter mile in such areas.

AURORA, COLORADO
Urban Street Standards

BUS ACCESS—It is required that bus routes and appropriate bus stop locations in the street network be identified in coordination with the Regional Transportation District (RTD) and city staff. Bus routes should be generally planned at a spacing of every half mile. All street intersections on the bus routes should be designed to allow adequate bus access.

Aurora, Colo., Mun. Code ch. 126, art. II, § 126-36.5(V)(G)(1)(d) (2009).

SAN DIEGO, CALIFORNIA | PLANNED DISTRICTS CHAPTER
Municipal Code

Locate transit stops to maximize access and optimize transit service and pedestrian and bikeway connections. Where located near crossroads and major activity centers, stops should be at one-quarter mile intervals.

San Diego, Cal., Mun. Code ch. 15, art. 14, div. 4, § 1514.0408(j)(1) (2009).

FIGURE 3-9

In a Superblock, Most Destinations Are More Than a Quarter Mile from a Through-Street

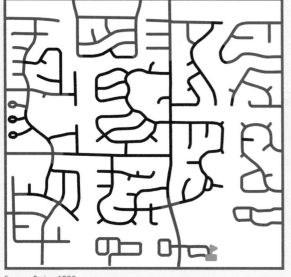

Source: Ewing 1996.

FIGURE 3-10

Transit Users Walking to Bus Stops

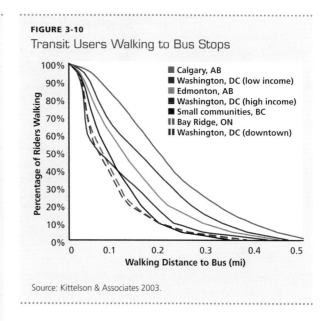

Source: Kittelson & Associates 2003.

Figure 3-10 shows the results of several studies of transit riders' walking distances to bus stops in North American cities. Although there is some variation between cities and income groups, the studies show that 75 to 80 percent of bus riders walk one-quarter mile or less. Although rail transit riders will walk farther, their numbers also drop off precipitously after a half mile (Cervero 1994, p. 180; Zhao et al. 2003, p. 36).

If a quarter to a half mile is a comfortable walking distance, it follows that transit routes may be no farther than a half mile apart to blanket a service area. This reasoning assumes that transit stops are closely spaced along routes, as they usually are in the United States (seven to ten stops per mile is the customary spacing). It also assumes that local streets lead directly to stops, as they usually do in urban settings. However, if stops are infrequent or local streets are curvilinear—both of which will increase walking distances—parallel routes must be even closer together to maintain reasonable walking access to transit.

This simple logic is the reason why many TOD manuals specify that collectors and arterials should be spaced no more than a half mile apart. Collectors and arterials are favored for transit service because they tend to have wider lanes and more direct routes, and they cover greater distances end-to-end than do local streets.

Half-mile spacing of higher-order streets is usually embraced not only for reasons of transit access but also to provide better access to commercial facilities (which are most often located on higher-order roads) and to discourage speeding on local streets (which occurs when it takes more than a minute to reach through-streets). For curvilinear street networks, the equivalent density is four centerline miles of through-streets per square mile of land area.

The importance of half-mile route spacing is demonstrated in an analysis of the comprehensive geographic growth in urban bus services nationwide during the 1970s (in response to a sudden infusion of federal funding). The analysis shows a lane mile per new rider elasticity of 0.86, across the 11 bus systems studied. In other words, for every 1 percent increase in geographic coverage, as measured by bus miles, there was an associated 0.86 percent increase in ridership (Pratt and Evans 2004).

A study of the travel characteristics in California transit-oriented developments further illustrates the need for closely spaced routes. According to the study (Evans et al. 2007), 27 percent of commuters living within one-half mile of a rail station take transit to get to work. For those living one-half mile to three miles from a station, however, that share falls to only 7 percent. For office workers within one-half mile of rail transit stations, transit commute shares average 19 percent. This figure is particularly impressive when compared with the region-wide average of 5 percent.

Of course, transit service quality depends on more than just geographic coverage. According to the *Transit Capacity and Quality of Service Manual* (Kittelson & Associates 2003), service frequency, hours of service, load factors, on-time performance, and travel time relative to the automobile are also important, and the manual contains quantitative standards for each of these measures.

Two- to Four-Lane Streets (with Rare Exceptions)

AS BLOCKS HAVE GOTTEN LONGER AND GRIDS HAVE GIVEN WAY to discontinuous, curvilinear street networks, the few remaining through-streets have had to be widened to carry the same volume of traffic. In suburban areas, a standard arterial cross section is now six lanes, with additional turn lanes at intersections. It is hard to find a six-lane arterial that is easy to cross, pleasant to walk along, or comfortable to wait next to when using transit.

The conventional theory of roadway design has been that wider, straighter, flatter, and more open thoroughfares are better from the standpoint of traffic safety. High-speed designs are presumed to be more forgiving of driver error and thus to lead to reduced incidence of crashes and injuries. As stated in *A Policy on Geometric Design of Highways and Streets*, often referred to as the "Green Book," "Every effort should be made to use as high a design speed as practical to attain a desired degree of safety" (AASHTO 2004b, pp. 66–67). Another standard of the transportation engineering field, the Transportation Research Board's *Highway Capacity Manual* (TRB 2000), bases roadway level-of-service determinations on speed along arterials and delay at intersections. Streets and intersections are widened in an unending effort to earn passing grades, without regard to the effects on development patterns or walkability (Ewing 1992, 1993).

Beginning with Jane Jacobs's (1961) *The Death and Life of Great American Cities* and extending to the new urbanism, smart growth, and similar design and planning movements, urban planners have argued for narrower, shorter, more enclosed, and more interconnected streets. The new urbanists seem to have gotten it right, not only from the standpoint of walkability but also from the perspective of traffic safety. It has long been understood that vehicle operating speeds decline as individual lanes and street sections are narrowed (see figure 3-11). The most recent research also shows that, in addition to slower speeds, drivers behave less aggressively on narrow streets, run fewer traffic signals, and are involved in fewer crashes with pedestrians, bicyclists, and other vehicles (Dumbaugh and Rae 2009).

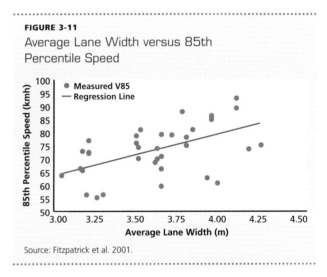

FIGURE 3-11

Average Lane Width versus 85th Percentile Speed

Source: Fitzpatrick et al. 2001.

On multilane streets, where passing is possible, high-speed drivers set the prevailing speed. On two-lane streets, prudent drivers set the pace and others must follow. One might expect, then, that reducing multilane roads to two lanes would result in slower and, perhaps, safer roadways. In fact, before-and-after studies of *road diet* projects (see sidebar) confirm this hypothesis, finding that traffic crashes decrease by as much as 34 percent as lanes are eliminated (Stout et al. 2006). Narrowing streets is also shown as an effective countermeasure to the most common pedestrian crashes (D. Burden and Lagerway 1999; Zegeer et al. 2002, p. 53).

The lower vehicle operating speeds and shorter crossing distances of narrow streets make them more comfortable for pedestrians. This increased level of comfort is confirmed by visual preference survey data (for example, Ewing et al. 2006), where the addition of travel lanes beyond the basic two is associated with lower preference scores. Hedonic price literature shows that residential real estate markets also favor narrow, slow-speed streets. Preferences for narrower streets are also demonstrated by how people vote with their feet, literally. One study by Untermann (1990) reports higher pedestrian volumes on narrow streets than on wide streets. Another study, from Orlando, Florida, shows how narrowing a roadway can increase pedestrian volumes (by 23 percent) and cycling rates (by 30 to 144 percent) (Rosales 2006). Narrower, low-volume streets are also associated with higher degrees of sociability among neighbors (Appleyard 1981). More elderly users, more bicyclists, more people out walking pets, and more pedestrians crossing back and forth all attest to a level of pedestrian comfort with traffic on the narrower streets.

Although two-lane streets are preferable, there are ways to make wider streets function like two-lane streets. By dividing four-lane streets, they become almost as easy to cross as two-lane streets. Raised medians or islands offer pedestrians protection halfway across and allow them to focus on one direction of traffic at a time. They thereby greatly reduce crossing delays at uncontrolled locations and reduce pedestrian crash rates—in some cases by as much as half—compared with undivided roadways or roadways with center two-way left-turn lanes (Bowman and Vecellio 1994). Raised medians are particularly important in suburbs, where long blocks encourage midblock crossings (S. Smith et al. 1987, pp. 61–62).

Another way to divide four-lane streets is to provide one-way pairs or couplets of two or three lanes in each direction. Rather than separating opposing traffic through the use of a raised median, the one-way pair separates opposing traffic with an entire active block face, complete with cross streets, between the pairs. Each street in the pair can be limited to two or three lanes and still carry heavy traffic volumes because of the

Road Diets

The term *road diet* refers to a type of road reconfiguration where four-lane roads are restriped to have two travel lanes (one in each direction), plus a center turn lane. Particularly in dense urban environments where right-of-way is limited, the technique can provide additional road space that might not otherwise be available for bike lanes, wider sidewalks, on-street parking, and pedestrian islands. Narrowing the amount of road space dedicated to travel lanes improves safety by reducing average vehicle travel speeds and by shortening the distance pedestrians must traverse when crossing the street. It also reduces rear-end and side-swipe vehicle crashes because left-turning vehicles that formerly had to wait in travel lanes before turning can now use the center turn lane (Huang, Stewart, and Zegeer 2002). Where the reconfiguration results in the creation of on-street parking, pedestrian safety and comfort are enhanced by having a row of cars between the travel lane and the sidewalk. The city of Fresno, California (2012), has pursued a number of road diet reconfigurations and maintains a comprehensive website on the technique.

Arterial before and after a road diet project (Collingwood, Ontario). | *Dan Burden*

ABOVE: **Two-lane street carrying 20,000 vehicles per day (Kirkland, Washington);** RIGHT: **Four-lane street carrying 24,000 vehicles per day (Bellevue, Washington).** | *Dan Burden*

efficiency of one-way streets (Ewing 2000b). A prominent example is downtown Portland, Oregon, where all the streets are paired, each one containing two or three lanes of one-way traffic. New urbanist Peter Calthorpe has been a proponent of one-way pairs and includes them in his town center designs.

Six-lane roads are best avoided in pedestrian areas. Where unavoidable, they are most comfortable for pedestrians when bordering buildings provide a sense of enclosure, when sidewalks are appropriately buffered from traffic by street trees or curbside parking, and when wide, raised, planted medians break up their paved expanse. Substantial trees in the median and on either side of the street have the power to visually divide street space in half, for a sense of visual enclosure and human scale.

An exception to this guideline is the multiway boulevard (A. Jacobs, Macdonald, and Rofe 2002). These boulevards are composed of four or more heavily trafficked through-lanes divided from local roads. The local roads, also known as *frontage roads* or *service roads*, run parallel to the through-lanes and are normally composed of one moving lane and one or two parking lanes. These roads allow vehicles access to the highway and to other local streets. Tree-covered medians separate the busier through-streets from the calmer local roads. In addition to trees, these medians also often include transit stops, bike paths, and benches.

BELOW: **A six-lane cross section with pedestrian-friendly features (Bethesda, Maryland);** RIGHT: **Half of a one-way couplet with pedestrian-friendly features (Portland, Oregon).** | *Reid Ewing*

PEDESTRIAN- AND TRANSIT-ORIENTED DESIGN

Number of Street Lanes

Although streets that are wider than two to four lanes pose considerable challenges for pedestrians, it is the rare community today that is able to do away entirely with the demand for such streets. The following provisions demonstrate two attempts to address this issue. Albuquerque's form-based code specifies the boulevard as the widest permissible street type, and the code provides a number of restrictions and controls to make those streets somewhat safer and more welcoming for pedestrians. By providing for one-way slip roads separated from the primary three or four lanes, the boulevard ensures that pedestrians walking along the right-of-way experience slower traffic and are buffered from the rapidly moving bulk of vehicular traffic. Additionally, the landscaped medians that separate the slip roads from traffic provide some protection for pedestrians who are crossing, ensuring that they need not make their way across so broad and inhospitable an expanse of roadway.

Oregon's administrative rule 660-012-0045(7) instructs local governments to establish standards to minimize excessive width requirements for streets, in order to reduce design speed and provide for the needs of pedestrians and bicyclists. The rule also balances emergency-vehicle requirements, a common source of concern for jurisdictions considering narrower streets. The rule is worded generally and could apply to both the width and number of lanes.

ALBUQUERQUE, NEW MEXICO
Form-Based Code

ABQ	BV-115	BV-125	BV-135
Thoroughfare Type	Boulevard	Boulevard	Boulevard
Right-of-Way Width	115 feet	125 feet	135 feet
Pedestrian Realm	15 feet, each side	13 feet, each side	13 feet, each side
Walkway Type	8 foot Sidewalk	8 foot Sidewalk	8 foot Sidewalk
Planter Type	5 foot Continuous planter	5 foot Continuous planter	5 foot Continuous planter
Landscape Type	Trees at 25' o.c. Avg.	Trees at 25' o.c. Avg.	Trees at 25' o.c. Avg.
Edge zone	2 feet	2 feet	2 feet
Roadway Realm	85 feet	80 feet	89 feet
Pavement Width	18 feet-33 feet-18 feet	18 feet-44 feet-18 feet	28 feet-33 feet-28 feet
Traffic Lanes	2 lanes w/ one turning lane & two one-way slip roads	4 lanes & two one-way slip roads	3 lanes, one turning lane & two one-way slip roads
Parking Lanes	8 feet	8 feet	8 feet
Curb Type	Curb	Curb	Curb
Radius	15 feet	25 feet	25 feet

Albuquerque, N.M., Code ch. 14, art. 16, § 14-16-3-22(C)(4)(d) (2009).

OREGON STATE
Administrative Rule

Local governments shall establish standards for local streets and accessways that minimize pavement width and total right-of-way consistent with the operational needs of the facility. The intent of this requirement is that local governments consider and reduce excessive standards for local streets and accessways in order to reduce the cost of construction, provide for more efficient use of urban land, provide for emergency vehicle access while discouraging inappropriate traffic volumes and speeds, and which accommodate convenient pedestrian and bicycle circulation.

Ore. Admin R. 660-012-0045(7) (2009).

Local street (Lake Oswego, Oregon). | *Dan Burden*

Octavia Boulevard in San Francisco, California, once a double-deck freeway, was transformed into a multiway boulevard designed to allow heavy traffic along its four-lane central roadway while permitting slower local traffic along the parallel service roads on each side of the central lanes (Macdonald 2006). The boulevard carries close to 50,000 vehicles per day.

The recommended cap of four lanes goes hand in hand with previously discussed guidelines calling for short blocks and frequent through-streets. Streets can be held to four lanes only if the street network is dense enough to handle the total volume of traffic (Ewing 2000b). In the tradeoff between more streets and wider streets, opt for the former in the interest of walkability.

Continuous Sidewalks Appropriately Scaled

AS AMERICAN SOCIETY HAS BECOME INCREASINGLY AUTO DEPENDENT, new streets have been built without sidewalks or with sidewalks on only one side. In a fit of circular reasoning, traffic engineers and real estate developers have argued against sidewalks on the grounds that no one will walk anyway. The engineers and developers are right in one sense—sidewalks by themselves will not induce walking. Other pedestrian-oriented features must be present in addition to sidewalks, which is one reason why this first reference to sidewalks as an urban design feature appears fairly late in the chapter.

Little quantitative evidence exists on the importance of sidewalks for walkability. Perhaps the connection is too obvious. What is known about sidewalks is mostly from direct observation. In her famous tribute to cities and city life, Jane Jacobs (1961, pp. 29–88) devotes a full three chapters to the importance of sidewalks, noting their ability to provide street security, promote neighborly contact, and ease the assimilation of children into adult society. These valuable roles are performed on top of their main function: serving as safe rights-of-way for pedestrians to travel between destinations.

To plan for such a multifunctional system, Ehrenfeucht and Loukaitou-Sideris (2010) recommend recognizing three distinct roles that sidewalks can and should play in a community: (1) as transportation infrastructure, (2) as spaces for everyday life, and (3) as leisure destinations. Viewing sidewalks in these multiple dimensions as a continuous and distinct urban network makes it easier to envision improvements to enhance these spaces. Part of creating a continuous sidewalk network using this approach includes the more prosaic improvements of filling in missing links in the network, fixing cracks, and installing curb cuts. But other improvements also become evident, such as planting and maintaining street trees and providing gathering places and space for informal activities, like street vending and performing (Ehrenfeucht and Loukaitou-Sideris 2010).

Attention to these details can influence not only community life, but also how often and how far people

Lack of sidewalks plagues suburbia (Port Charlotte and Orlando, Florida).
| *Kelly Morphy; Reid Ewing*

Clear width of five feet allows space between passing pedestrians (Berkeley, California). | *Reid Ewing*

are willing to walk. In one survey (Agrawal, Schlossberg, and Irvin 2008), 87 percent of respondents listed sidewalk condition as an important factor in their decision of whether to make a trip on foot. A cross-sectional analysis of walking, sociodemographics, and environmental variables in the state of Washington similarly found continuous sidewalks significantly related to walking (Moudon et al. 2007). In Portland, Oregon, researchers measuring sidewalk continuity, crosswalk frequency, street continuity, and topography found that neighborhoods that ranked high for these features had three to four times the number of pedestrians, bicyclists, and transit users as low-ranking neighborhoods (1000 Friends of Oregon 1993).

Sidewalk availability is also implicated in pedestrian safety: a cross-sectional study of urban streets with and without sidewalks found that in residential and mixed residential areas, crashes involving pedestrians were more than two times as likely to occur in areas without sidewalks than would be expected on the basis of exposure alone (Knoblauch et al. 1988). Similarly, analysis of California's Safe Routes to School program found appreciable increases in perceptions of pedestrian safety and sidewalk use associated with projects to fill in gaps in the sidewalk networks near elementary schools (Boarnet et al. 2005).

Not surprisingly, this link to actual and perceived safety is also connected to public health, with a number of studies

FIGURE 3-12

One Set of Sidewalk Warrants

Arterials/collectors	Both sides
Local streets commercial areas	Both sides
Local streets residential areas	
More than 4 units per acre	Both sides
1–4 units per acre	One side
Fewer than 1 unit per acre	None

Source: Knoblauch et al. 1988, p. 143.

showing a positive association between the presence and condition of sidewalks and physical activity among children and adults (Diez Roux and Mair 2010; Handy 2005; Heath et al. 2006; Kaczynski 2010; Krahnstover-Davison and Lawson 2006; McMillan 2005).

A focus on sidewalks at a network level makes it clear that creating isolated islands or oases for pedestrians is

Sidewalks should be scaled to the amount of traffic they handle (Amarillo, Texas; Edmonton, Alberta). | *Melissa Dailey; Dan Burden*

Sidewalk Widths

Knoxville's code calls for a ten-foot-wide sidewalk on both sides of the street. The sidewalks include a five-foot planting zone, which provides a buffer between pedestrians and traffic, particularly in combination with the parking lane. Seattle requires a minimum 12-foot-wide sidewalk, broad enough for considerable pedestrian traffic and for couples to pass one another.

KNOXVILLE, TENNESSEE | SOUTH WATERFRONT DEVELOPMENT CODE

Streetscape Standards

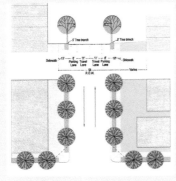

- **THOROUGHFARE TYPE:** Commercial street, CS-58-38-2PL-BR
- **RIGHT-OF-WAY WIDTH:** 58'
- **PAVEMENT WIDTH:** 38'
- **MOVEMENT:** Slow movement
- **DESIGN SPEEDS:** 25 mph
- **PEDESTRIAN CROSSING TIME:** 10.3 seconds
- **TRAFFIC LANES:** 2 lanes
- **PARKING LANES:** Both sides @ 8' marked
- **BIKE LANES:** na
- **CURB RADIUS:** 15'
- **WALKWAY TYPE:** 10' sidewalk
- **PLANTER TYPE:** 5' continuous trench
- **CURB TYPE:** Curb
- **LANDSCAPE TYPE:** Trees @ 30' O.C.
- **TRANSPORTATION PROVISION:** Bus route
- **UTILITIES:** All underground

Knoxville, Tenn., Ordinance O-29-07 (February 27, 2007) (adopted as part of the city code by Knoxville, Tenn., Code appendix B, art. 4, § 4.1 (2009)).

SEATTLE, WASHINGTON

Land Use Code

The owner shall construct a sidewalk no less than twelve (12) feet in width.

Seattle, Wash., Mun. Code tit. 23, subtit. 3, div. 3, ch. 23.71, § 23.71.008(E)(1) (2009).

insufficient. Pedestrian networks must be as continuous as the street networks that are built and maintained for motorists. To this end, the sidewalk warrants system of the Federal Highway Administration calls for sidewalks on all streets except local ones in low-density residential areas (see figure 3-12).

As to sidewalk width, design is dictated by the intensity of surrounding land uses, the anticipated demand for nonwalking activities, and the dimensions of the human body. Given the existence of body sway, as well as the desire to avoid contact with others, Fruin (1971, p. 20) suggests the typical "body ellipse" is 61 centimeters (24 inches) by 46 centimeters (18 inches) for moving persons. Hence, a five-foot sidewalk is wide enough for two people to walk comfortably abreast, or a person in a wheelchair to turn around, and is thus a good dimension where pedestrian traffic is light, street furniture is limited, and buildings are set back from the sidewalk, such as in a residential neighborhood. Where these conditions are not met, as in any respectable downtown, wider sidewalks are warranted. This bit of conventional wisdom is confirmed by visual preference surveys, where wider sidewalks in commercial areas receive higher scores than narrower examples (Ewing et al. 2005).

For strolling couples to pass one another without awkward maneuvering takes about 12 feet of clear sidewalk width. An extra 2.5 feet may be required if street furniture is plentiful (Pushkarev and Zupan 1975, pp. 151–52). An additional one to 1.5 feet of sidewalk width is required if buildings run up to the sidewalk, because of the tendency of pedestrians to maintain this "shy" distance from walls (Fruin 1971, p. 44). An additional 10–15 feet may be warranted at high-volume transit stops to accommodate queuing and shelters at the curb (Paumier 2004, p. 84). Stucki (2003), synthesizing the

FIGURE 3-13

Recommended Sidewalk Widths in High-Volume Locations

Author	Recommendation
Alexander, Ishikawa, and Silverstein	12 feet minimum; 20 feet maximum
Untermann	8–9 feet minimum; 12 feet desirable
S. Smith et al.	12–15 feet
Whyte	15 feet minimum; 30 feet typical maximum
Calthorpe	15–20 feet
Sucher	12 feet

Sources: Alexander, Ishikawa, and Silverstein 1977; Calthorpe 1993; S. Smith et al. 1987; Sucher 1995; Untermann 1984; Whyte 1988.

work of Ulrich Weidmann, arrives at shy distances for different obstacles: approximately 1.5 feet from walls, or one foot from fences, streetlights, trees, and benches. Given such considerations, it is easy to see why some leading urban designers have recommended sidewalk widths of 10, 15, and even 20 feet for high-volume locations (see figure 3-13).

Just as streets are scaled to vehicular traffic volumes, so should sidewalks be scaled to pedestrian traffic volumes. Sidewalks should be wide enough to accommodate pedestrian traffic without crowding, yet not so wide as to appear empty most of the time. A hint of

crowding may actually add to the vitality and interest of a street. For this reason, some urban designers recommend maximum sidewalk widths, as well as minimums (see figure 3-13).

To allow walking at near-normal speeds, sidewalks should provide at least 25 square feet per pedestrian at peak times (Fruin 1971, pp. 42, 47–50). More space is required, perhaps 40 square feet per person, to permit maneuvering around slower pedestrians and to avoid oncoming and crossing pedestrians. All hint of crowding is eliminated at 100 to 150 square feet per person, though the street will still appear lively at this pedestrian density.

Safe Crossings

IN A GOOD WALKING ENVIRONMENT, a high degree of interplay occurs between opposite sides of the street and between adjacent blocks. Shoppers, residents, and other users engage in activities on one side of the street and then the other, or in one block and then the next. The easier a street is to cross, the better a street functions for both pedestrians and the businesses that front the street. Pedestrian movement back and forth makes drivers behave more cautiously, which in turn makes streets easier to cross. The two phenomena reinforce each other.

Research shows that appropriate crossing improvements increase pedestrian volumes (Boarnet et al. 2005; Harkey and Zegeer 2004; Knoblauch, Nitzburg, and Seifert 2001). Evidence and observation suggest that for pedestrian comfort and safety, crossings should be frequent and well marked (Fitzpatrick, Ullman, and Trout 2004). Pedestrian crossing opportunities should be available every 300 feet or so along the street and should be located according to pedestrian-desired lines, for example, at a school or transit station, or where a trail or alley intersects the street.

All approaches to signal- or stop sign–controlled intersections should have marked crosswalks to channel

pedestrians to common crossing points, to alert drivers to the possibility of pedestrians, and perhaps to slow traffic. Even with these features, some crossings will invariably be located at uncontrolled locations, whether at intersections without controls or midblock locations. Research shows that marked crosswalks may actually increase vehicle–pedestrian collisions on higher-volume streets and that additional *crossing enhancements* are needed (Chu, Guttenplan, and Kourtellis 2007) (see figure 3-14).

The simplest but least effective crossing enhancements are warning signs, flashing warning lights, and high-visibility crosswalk markings. The *Manual on Uniform Traffic Control Devices* (*MUTCD*) directs that "because nonintersection pedestrian crossings are generally unexpected by the road user, warning signs … should be installed and adequate visibility should be provided by parking prohibitions." (FHWA 2003, p. 3B-28).

In addition, at locations where pedestrian crossings are not expected, the *MUTCD* suggests the use of high-visibility pavement markings. High visibility is achieved with diagonal or longitudinal marking patterns as opposed to standard transverse parallel lines. There is some question of whether simple transverse lines should be used anywhere, as they are often mistaken for stop lines, causing motorists to pull up into the crosswalk area rather than

....

FIGURE 3-14

Safety of Marked versus Unmarked Crosswalks

Lanes	ADT	Median	Marked Crosswalk	Unmarked Crossing
1-2	All	Without	Equally safe	Equally safe
3+	<12,000	With or without	Equally safe	Equally safe
3+	12,000–15,000	Without	Safer	Less safe
3+	12,000–15,000	With	Less safe	Safer
3+	>15,000	With or without	Less safe	Safer

Source: Zegeer et al. 2005.

Note: ADT = average daily traffic.

maintain proper distance. At whatever location in whatever configuration, greater visibility can be achieved with extrawide stripes, up to 24 inches wide.

The *MUTCD* suggests placing stop lines (also known as *stop bars*) for motorists a minimum of four feet in advance of crosswalks. Four feet is not enough separation for a pedestrian street, particularly a multilane street. The farther motorists stop from a crosswalk, the better motorists and pedestrians can see and avoid each other. When a vehicle stops too close to a crosswalk, it can obscure the view of pedestrians for motorists in adjacent lanes. Research demonstrates that advance stop lines increase the average distance that motorists stop in front of crosswalks and thus reduce the likelihood of motorists intruding into crosswalks. Advance stop lines may be placed ten, 20, or even 30 feet from crosswalks.

On multilane streets, a raised median or pedestrian crossing island will facilitate pedestrian crossings. Raised medians allow pedestrians to deal with one direction of traffic at a time, and to cross halfway rather than having to wait for a gap in traffic in both directions. Raised

medians also significantly reduce pedestrian collision rates on multilane urban arterials. Where continuous medians are infeasible, short crossing islands can substitute (Ewing and King 2002, p. 28). Short, squat crossing islands are actually superior from the standpoint of traffic calming as they introduce horizontal deflection into travel. The next upgrade in enhancing street crossings is the introduction of curb extensions, or *bulbouts*. Curb extensions assist pedestrians by shortening crossing distances and increasing pedestrian visibility by elevating pedestrians slightly. They also provide space for landscaping and signage that draw attention to crosswalks. And if a street is really choked down, curb extensions slow traffic somewhat.

More aggressive forms of traffic calming, such as raised crosswalks or raised intersections, are likely to be more effective as crossing enhancements than are curb extensions. A study of driver yielding behavior at crosswalks in Cambridge, Massachusetts, found that more than half the motorists yielded to pedestrians after raised crosswalks and raised intersections were installed, compared with fewer than 20 percent before installation.

The ultimate pedestrian crossing enhancement is a pedestrian-activated signal. When pedestrian-activated signals are deployed, driver compliance with yield

UPPER LEFT: **Pedestrian crossing island (Asheville, North Carolina);** LOWER LEFT: **Advance stop line at an uncontrolled crossing (Laguna Beach, California);** ABOVE: **Raised median facilitating a midblock crossing (Terre Haute, Indiana).** | *Dan Burden (upper left and above); Reid Ewing (lower left)*

LEFT: **Curb extensions necking down an intersection (Easton Village, Ohio); BELOW: Pedestrian-activated signal (Tokyo, Japan)** | *Dan Burden; Reid Ewing*

requirements rises to nearly 100 percent. No other traffic-calming or traffic-control device is likely to be sufficient on high-volume, high-speed arterials where gaps in traffic are infrequent.

To encourage crossing at designated crosswalks, and to discourage jaywalking, pedestrian delays at signalized intersections should be kept to a minimum. Research has shown that pedestrians start exhibiting risk-taking behavior (for example, jaywalking or running across the street) when their delay exceeds 30 seconds. Therefore, signal cycles should be kept relatively short, certainly no longer than 90 seconds. Signals should be pretimed in most cases to provide walking phases automatically, without motor vehicle or pedestrian activation.

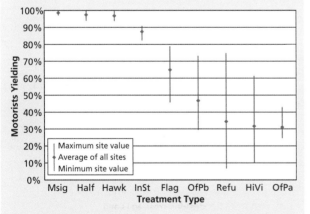

FIGURE 3-15

Average and Range of Motorists Yielding to Pedestrians by Crossing Treatment

Maximum site value
Average of all sites
Minimum site value

Motorists Yielding

Treatment Type: Msig Half Hawk InSt Flag OfPb Refu HiVi OfPa

Source: Fitzpatrick et al. 2006, p. 49.

Note: Msig = midblock signal; Half = half signal; Hawk = HAWK signal beacon; InSt = in-street crossing signs; Flag = pedestrian crossing flags; OfPb = overhead flashing beacons (push-button activation); Refu = median refuge island; HiVi = high visibility signs and markings; OfPa = overhead flashing beacons (passive activation).

Shorter cycles and pretimed signals are consistent with low-speed traffic progression, the desired condition on pedestrian streets.

At key intersections with large numbers of pedestrians, consideration should be given to leading pedestrian intervals (LPIs), which give pedestrians time to cross before parallel traffic gets its green light, or *pedestrian scrambles* (also referred to as *Barnes Dances*), which stop vehicle traffic in all directions and allow pedestrians to cross in any fashion, including diagonally. In one study, LPIs were found to reduce vehicle–pedestrian collision severity by 64 percent (King 1999). In another, LPIs reduced the number of vehicle–pedestrian conflicts to nearly zero (Van Houten et al. 2000). In a third, pedestrian scrambles reduced pedestrian collisions by 51 percent (Chen, Chen, and Ewing 2012). Limitations on vehicle turning movements can also improve pedestrian safety at street corners. One-fifth of motor vehicle collisions at signalized intersections involve a turning vehicle striking a pedestrian. Right turns on red and large curb corner radii both create hazards for pedestrians crossing side streets: the large radii allow for higher-speed turning movements, whereas right turns on red tend to focus driver attention on traffic entering the intersection from the left instead of on crossing pedestrians. Eliminating right turns on red and shortening corner radii, particularly where pedestrian traffic is heavy, can contribute to a safer pedestrian environment.

LEFT: **Wide corner with free right turn (Columbia, Maryland)**; ABOVE: **Tight corner with no right turn on red (Bethesda, Maryland).** | *Reid Ewing*

One final issue with regard to crossing safety is the type of curb ramp employed. Basic requirements for curb ramps are specified in the *ADA Accessibility Guidelines for Buildings and Facilities* (U.S. Access Board 2002). These guidelines specify ramp slope, width, land-ing dimensions, and detectable warnings, but not the type of ramp that should be used. The basic choice is between type 1 ramps, which are diagonal to the cross streets and type 2 ramps, which are perpendicular to the cross streets. The preferred design is a type 2 ramp

LOCAL CODE EXAMPLES

Safe Pedestrian Crossings

Aurora, Colorado's street standards require consideration of midblock pedestrian crossings in all locations where pedestrians are likely to be numerous. The requirement is situated in the context of an integrated series of provi-sions providing for safe crossings at intersections and midblock locations. Those provisions also include a hierarchy of crosswalk treatments, signage requirements, and other features. Importantly, the Aurora standard discourages midblock crossings where signals are absent. The Kansas City, Missouri, subdivision code also calls for midblock crossings, in this case for blocks longer than 900 feet. In contrast with the Aurora standards, however, the code provides for no other safety features. This lack may prove to be insufficient for adequate crossing safety.

AURORA, COLORADO
Urban Street Standards

MIDBLOCK CROSSING. Midblock crossings with curb extensions should be considered at locations where a substantial number of pedestrians or bicyclists attempt to cross streets regardless of the presence of protection or identification of the crossing. These circumstances typically occur in locations with pedestrian attractions on both sides of a roadway, in areas with a combination of street-facing retail shops and on-street parking, and the presence of long blocks (i.e., blocks of 600-feet or greater). Midblock crossing will only be applied to limited locations and will be analyzed on a case by case basis. Multilane un-signalized controlled mid-block crossing should be avoided.

Aurora, Colo., Mun. Code ch. 126, art. II, § 126-36.5(V)(G)(2)(g) (2009).

KANSAS CITY, MISSOURI
Subdivision Code

Pedestrian ways or crosswalks not less than ten feet in width shall be provided near the center and entirely across any block which is 900 feet or more in length where deemed essential in the opin-ion of the city plan commission to provide adequate pedestrian circulation or access to schools, shopping centers, churches, parks or transportation facilities. At the time of preliminary plat approval, this requirement may be modified in an instance where this access is adequately served otherwise.

Kansas City, Mo., Code of Ord. § 66-124(a)(2) (2009).

that is in line with the crosswalk. This type shortens the crossing distance and helps align visually impaired people with the opposite side of the street.

Bridgeport Way in University Place, Washington, offers a good example of a crosswalk improvement on a high-volume arterial in a suburban setting. The original street, a five-lane arterial with no provision for pedestrians or bicyclists, was narrowed to four lanes and redesigned to include warning signs, advance stop lines, flashing inset lights, a median crossing island, and a pedestrian-activated signal. There are now 59 percent fewer pedestrian crashes along the street than before the improvements were made.

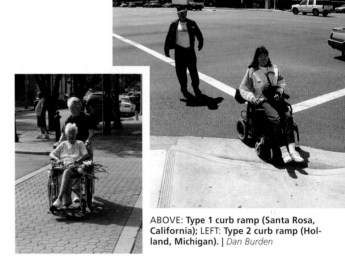

ABOVE: **Type 1 curb ramp (Santa Rosa, California)**; LEFT: **Type 2 curb ramp (Holland, Michigan).** | *Dan Burden*

Appropriate Buffering from Traffic

NOT LONG AGO, PLANNERS AND DESIGNERS THOUGHT IT WISE to completely separate pedestrians from automobile traffic. Pedestrian pathways were built through open spaces of planned communities. Pedestrian malls were created by closing off downtown streets.

The origin of this paradigm dates at least as far back as the General Motors "Futurama" Pavilion, designed by industrial designer Norman Bel Geddes for the 1939 New York World's Fair. Bel Geddes designed a future where pedestrian sidewalks would be elevated high above cars (which would be located on the ground level) because, in his words, "danger lies where paths cross" (as quoted in Leinberger 2008, p. 18).

This *separatist* view of vehicle and pedestrian systems has been eclipsed. Pedestrians and automobiles are now thought to belong in the same environment, each providing natural surveillance and supportive activity for the other. Street-adjacent sidewalks have been installed in planned communities that once relied on off-street pathways, and pedestrian-only streets have been re-opened to automobile traffic. This change in viewpoint does not mean that pedestrians and automobiles can be on top of each other, only that they can coexist happily with the right degree of separation and buffering.

In rare instances, pedestrians and automobiles can literally share space. Where a positive mix of the two exists, and pedestrians dominate (as on some college

LEFT: **Positive mix of pedestrians and traffic (Pasadena, California)**; BELOW: **Dangerous mix of pedestrians and traffic (Paris, France).** | *Dan Burden; Stock photo*

Woonerf

A *woonerf* (singular of *woonerven*) is a street designed to be shared by many users—those in cars as well as those on foot or bicycle. The term, which is Dutch, refers to a "living street" where most or all of the space is shared by all users. This design uses fewer divisions or demarcations of the street (such as through the use of curbs) to indicate reserved areas for particular users. In most cases, alternative street surfaces (for example, pavers) are used to emphasize the shared quality of the space. The intent is to create safe areas where children can play, bicyclists can ride, pedestrians can stroll, residents can sit, neighbors can chat, and … cars can move slowly and park. The five criteria for *woonerven*, originally articulated by Appleyard (1981) and now repeated in most design guides, are that they contain "gateways that announce that one has entered the woonerf; curves to slow vehicle traffic; amenities such as trees and play equipment that serve the dual purpose of forcing vehicles to slow down; no curbs; and intermittent parking so that cars do not form a wall of steel between the roadway and houses" (StreetsWiki 2012).

campuses and at some tourist destinations), minimal separation may be required (A. Jacobs 1993, p. 273). Where streets are traffic-calmed to *woonerf* standards, as occurs mostly in Europe, no separation is required at all (see sidebar). Even in American suburbs, where culs-de-sac are very short, sidewalks may be unnecessary since automobile traffic is infrequent and slow moving.

More often, pedestrians will not be comfortable without a separation between themselves and automobiles. A pedestrian level-of-service (LOS) measure developed by Bruce Landis et al. (2001) serves as the basis for multimodal LOS measurement in Florida (FDOT 2002, pp. 20–21). Landis et al.'s measure is based on participant ratings of walking conditions on a sample of roadways. Their pedestrian LOS model incorporates statistically significant roadway and traffic variables that capture pedestrians' perception of safety or comfort in the roadway environment. Pedestrian LOS varies with lateral separation between pedestrians and motor vehicles (+),

traffic volume (–), traffic speeds (–), and driveway frequency (–).

Design speeds, such as those established for different street types in *Best Development Practices* (Ewing 1996, p. 67), are the safe speeds at which traffic naturally travels. They are distinct from posted speeds, which tend to be set lower than design speeds and are, accordingly, ignored by many motorists. Because of the connection between design speeds and actual driving behavior, they provide a good basis for setting thresholds beyond which greater pedestrian separation and buffering are required.

At low design speeds, parked cars can serve as a metal buffer between the sidewalk and street. They slow traffic by narrowing the travel way and by creating *side friction* as they pull in and out parking spaces. In a visual preference survey (Ewing et al. 2005), the proportion of street frontage occupied by parked cars has the strongest influence on main-street scores of any of the variables tested: the higher the proportion of parked cars, the higher the main-street scores.

At higher design speeds, a row of street trees in the planting strip can serve as a buffer (see chapter 4, "Closely Spaced Shade Trees"). Planting strip width is more than just an aesthetic issue in cold climates. Snow is piled in this zone as it is plowed from the street, keeping it from blocking the sidewalk. Northern cities like Toronto have minimum widths for these strips to ensure adequate space for trees plus the piled snow. On urban streets with vertical curbs and moderate design speeds, trees can be planted within 1.5 feet of the curb without violating "Green Book" guidelines (AASHTO 2004b).

Street furniture, trees, and parked cars create a buffer from traffic (Manitou Springs, Colorado). | *Dan Burden*

Eliminate the curb while maintaining a moderate design speed, and trees may still be near the street edge. Raise the design speed and all bets are off (see figure 3-16).

Buffering created with parked cars, street trees, street furniture, or some combination not only increases pedestrian comfort and safety but adds to perceptions of street enclosure, human scale, complexity, coherence, and linkage (see chapter 2). These synergies can translate into higher levels of pedestrian activity, as demonstrated by Marshall, Garrick, and Hansen (2008, p. 51), who find that commercial centers with on-street parking and other compatible characteristics record more than six times the number of pedestrians as centers that lack these traits.

Interestingly, buffering also appears to increase safety for motorists. Dumbaugh's (2006a) analysis of the impacts of roadside design on single-vehicle crashes (into poles, trees, and parked cars) finds that the highest

LOCAL CODE EXAMPLES: Pedestrian Buffers

The Louisville, Kentucky, land development code requires a minimum sidewalk width of seven feet that includes a streetscape zone that buffers the pedestrian zone from traffic. The pedestrian zone must be a minimum of four feet wide, and if fewer than five feet, it must include frequent wider areas to allow two wheelchairs to pass each other. The streetscape zone has no specific size requirement, except when trees are present. The code provides considerable flexibility regarding the contents of the streetscape zone, allowing trees and other landscaping, street furniture, transit stops, and other uses. Because there are no firm requirements, this flexibility could lead to a narrow and barren streetscape zone. However, the wide minimum sidewalk size makes it likely that the streetscape zone will function as a barrier even when other features are not included in the zone.

The Provincetown, Massachusetts, code also explicitly calls for a buffer zone, which must be a minimum of ten feet wide and must visually separate parking from the road. Plantings are required, and the code calls for a sufficient setback from the road to limit traffic visibility hazards.

LOUISVILLE, KENTUCKY
Land Development Code

Sidewalks shall be at least 84" wide measured from the face of curb to the building façade, shall include a pedestrian zone and a streetscape zone, and may include a storefront zone.

1. PEDESTRIAN ZONE. The pedestrian zone is that portion of the sidewalk that is maintained free of any obstructions to allow for the passage of pedestrians. The pedestrian zone shall be at least 48 inches wide and shall not be shared with the streetscape or storefront zones. If the width of the pedestrian zone is less than five feet wide for more than 50 linear feet, passing spaces must be provided at intervals of no less than 200 feet apart and must provide an area of at least five feet by five feet to allow two wheelchairs to pass each other.

2. STREETSCAPE ZONE. That portion of the sidewalk located between the curb line and the Pedestrian Zone in which the following elements are located, following authorization by the Public Works Department:

- Street trees/grates, planting strips, raised planters
- Street light standards
- Street signs/pedestrian wayfinding signs
- Transit stops
- Media boxes
- Postal/freight collection boxes
- Parking meters
- Utility boxes/public phones/fire protection
- Seating (with/without tables)
- Trash receptacles
- Public art/water feature
- Bike racks

The Streetscape Zone shall be at least 48" wide when trees are included.

Louisville, Ky., Land Dev. Code § 5.8.1(C)(1)(b) (2009).

PROVINCETOWN, MASSACHUSETTS
Zoning Bylaws

A landscaped buffer strip at least 10' wide continuous except for approved driveways shall be established adjacent to any public road to visually separate parking and other uses from the road and which shall be planted with medium height plant materials set back a sufficient distance at intersections to prevent any traffic visibility hazard.

Provincetown, Mass., Zoning Bylaws art. 4, § 4053(2)(a) (2009).

FIGURE 3-16

Three Sets of Recommended Buffer Characteristics and Widths

	AASHTO	ASCE/NAHB/ULI	ITE
Curbing	Vertical curbs (local streets and collectors); vertical curbs outside shoulders in heavily developed areas (arterials)	Vertical or mountable curbs at higher densities (local streets and collectors)	Vertical curbs (except on local streets at low densities)
Minimum buffer/ planting strip	2', where strips are provided; where not provided, sidewalks should be 2' wider than normal	3–5' desirable (applies mainly to collectors)	5–6' (local streets) 10' (residential collectors) 5–10' (other major streets)
Minimum tree/ obstacle clearance	1.5' with vertical curbs; rural standards apply in absence of curbs	3' (local streets and collectors)	1–5' (with vertical curbs) 7' (with mountable curbs)

Sources: AASHTO 2004; ITE Technical Council Committee 5A-25A 1984, 1993; Residential Streets Task Force 1990.

Note: AASHTO = American Association of State Highway and Transportation Officials; ASCE = American Society of Civil Engineers; NAHB = National Association of Home Builders; ITE = Institute of Transportation Engineers; ULI = Urban Land Institute.

crash rates are associated with wide paved shoulders, whereas the lowest rate is tied to *livable streets*—those with trees, street furniture, and other features intended to provide a buffer for adjacent pedestrians. The reason for the rather paradoxical result is that off-the-road crashes are predominantly caused by excessive speed and turning maneuvers. Paved shoulders and other roadside treatments that remove obstacles from the roadside reduce *visual friction*—the perception of nearby objects—which induces faster vehicle speeds. Livable streets, on the other hand, increase visual friction by placing buffer-related objects close to the travel lane, which reduces vehicle speed, making it safer for both motorists and pedestrians alike.

Street-Oriented Buildings

THE GROWING DOMINANCE OF THE AUTOMOBILE has been accompanied by changes in architecture and site planning that cause buildings to relate poorly to streets. Buildings have spread out rather than up; they have stepped back from the street and have had their windows and doors reduced and reoriented away from the street. These changes have minimal negative effect on motorists as they whiz by. In fact, there is evidence that such features contribute to faster vehicle speeds (Marshall, Garrick, and Hansen 2008). But pity the pedestrian who doesn't have anything interesting to look at, feels cut off from building occupants, and has to walk through exposed parking lots.

In designing buildings for automobiles, tradeoffs have been made that subordinate the ease, convenience, safety, and enjoyment of pedestrians (Dumbaugh 2006b). Chief among the qualities that have been sacrificed are visual enclosure, transparency, and linkage (see chapter 2). A fourth change in building design—the increased mass of buildings as viewed from the street (that is, the increased width and sometimes height)—is less destructive to the streetscape and so is addressed later, as a secondary feature of pedestrian-oriented design.

When streets are lined with appropriately scaled, street-oriented buildings, a primary design objective is met: the creation of a reciprocal relationship between the private space on the interior of the structure and the

Turning toward the street (Kentlands, Maryland). | *Steven Mouzon*

public space in the right-of-way, particularly along the sidewalk.

In environments where this relationship is strong, the interactions, both physical and visual, between the interior private spaces and the exterior public spaces are smooth and relatively unimpeded. Assuming one is invited into the private space—because it is either a retail-oriented business or the home of a friend—one can move seamlessly through a *privacy transect*, across a range of zones from the fully public area of the sidewalk, through semipublic or semiprivate areas (such as the frontyard or outdoor seating or display area, the stoop, and the entrance threshold), into the private rooms of the building's interior (for example, the living room or the retail display area).

In his handbook on urban design, Seattle developer David Sucher (2003, p. 45) writes: "The key decision is the position of the building with respect to the sidewalk. This decision determines whether you have a city or a suburb." In cities, at least with respect to nonresidential structures, Sucher offers three rules: (1) build to the sidewalk (that is, the property line), (2) make building fronts "permeable" (that is, no blank walls), and (3) prohibit parking lots in front of buildings.

The auto-induced changes in building design and siting, described at the beginning of this section, may have evoked images of commercial strips, suburban office buildings in park-like settings, or inward-oriented shopping malls surrounded by parking. But the same influences have also been at work in residential areas. With suburbanization, houses first moved back from

FIGURE 3-18

Height-to-Width Ratios for Visual Enclosure

Alexander, Ishikawa, and Silverstein	1:1 ideal
Lynch and Hack	1:4 minimum; 1:2–1:3 ideal
Hedman	1:1–1:2 ideal
Duany and Plater-Zyberk	1:6 minimum
Allan Jacobs	1:2 minimum; 1:1 ideal

Sources: Alexander, Ishikawa, and Silverstein 1977; Duany and Plater-Zyberk 1992; Hedman 1984, p. 76; A. Jacobs 1993, p. 279; Lynch and Hack 1984, p. 158.

the street and assumed ranch-home proportions. Later, as the price of improved land forced the downsizing of lots, houses moved back closer to the street and assumed narrower and deeper proportions. This time, however, houses approached the street garage-first (Southworth and Owens 1993). Sometimes called *snout houses*, this building style discards the elements that had once linked houses to the street—windows, doors, entrance walks, porches, and balconies—in favor of wide driveways and garage doors (Hayden and Wark 2004). Urban design manuals confront this trend by requiring the primary entrances of dwelling units to be closest to the street.

The principle of visual enclosure can be used to tailor building setbacks to street width. Visual enclosure of streetscapes occurs when bordering buildings are tall enough in relation to street width to occupy most of a pedestrian's field of view (see chapter 2). The term *outdoor room* is sometimes applied to streetscapes that are so visually enclosed as to be room-like. The *walls* of the room are the vertical elements that bound and shape

FIGURE 3-17

Mall Connected to the Street through the Addition of Outbuildings

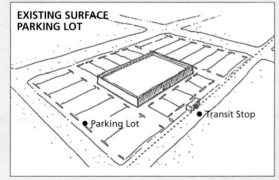
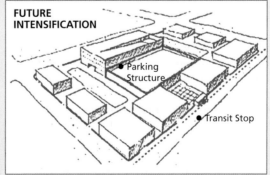

EXISTING SURFACE PARKING LOT

FUTURE INTENSIFICATION

Parking Structure

Parking Lot

Transit Stop

Transit Stop

Source: Calthorpe 1993, p. 111, reprinted by permission of the publisher.

CHECKLIST OF ESSENTIAL FEATURES

street spaces, usually buildings and closely planted street trees.

Experts disagree on the height-to-width ratio required for intensely experienced three-dimensional space (see figure 3-18). A common rule of thumb is that viewers should not be farther from the defining street edge than three times the enclosure height. This rule of thumb implies a minimum height-to-width ratio of 1:3.

For a residential street with a 40-foot right-of-way and 20-foot-high dwellings along it, the maximum front setback for a 1:3 height-to-width ratio would be ten feet. If a commercial street with a 60-foot right-of-way has 20-foot-tall storefronts built along it, they must sit directly on the right-of-way line (that is, at the sidewalk).

As streets get wider, the buildings alongside the road must rise to contain the space. At some point, however, even tall buildings will not do the job and street trees can be used to supplement (see chapter 4, "Closely Spaced Shade Trees"). Alternatively, street vistas can be punctuated by strong markers, such as civic monuments or prominent building facades. These focal points achieve a sense of visual enclosure by providing intangible boundaries rather than physical borders to the space (see chapter 5, "Public Art"). When a street is not strongly defined by buildings, focal points at its ends can maintain the visual linearity of the arrangement.

In addition to providing a sense of enclosure, focal points and street-oriented buildings can also create

CLOCKWISE FROM ABOVE: **Street with a 10:1 height-to-width ratio (New York, New York); Street with a 2:1 height-to-width ratio (Rome, Italy); Street with a 1:1 height-to-width ratio (Frankfort, Kentucky); Street with a 1:3 height-to-width ratio (Sebring, Florida).** | *Reid Ewing*

a safer pedestrian environment by communicating to drivers that greater caution is warranted. These design features can result in reductions in both vehicle speed and crash incidence (Dumbaugh and Li 2011). A study by Ivan, Garrick, and Hansen (2009) comparing roadway segments with different roadside characteristics finds that the presence of urban roadside features, such as buildings located adjacent to the street, is associated with speed reductions of up to ten miles per hour. Another study by Naderi, Kweon, and Maghelal (2008) finds that trees along a suburban collector roadway make people perceive it to be safer and also reduce vehicle speeds by three miles per hour, on average.

To create the sense of enclosure that pedestrians clearly prefer, cities and towns have begun using form-based codes. Building-form standards (a central element of form-based codes) control the alignment of buildings on the street; how close buildings are to sidewalks; the visibility and accessibility of building entrances; minimum lot-front coverage; minimum amounts of window coverage on facades; and physical elements required on buildings, such as stoops, porches, and types of balconies permitted. In contrast to conventional zoning that establishes minimum building setbacks, form-based codes often prescribe build-to lines close to front property lines at which some or all building facades are required to align.

LOCAL CODE

EXAMPLES ## Street-Oriented Buildings

Both Fort Worth, Texas, and Louisville, Kentucky, have encouraged street-oriented buildings by ensuring that buildings can be accessed from the streets they abut. These requirements counter the common situation in which retail stores can be entered only from their parking lots, which may be located to the side or rear of the building. Fort Worth's code requires that primary entrances face the street, except where a public space adjoins a building. Louisville's code also requires that the primary entrance be oriented toward the street or public open space. Where the primary entrance faces a public space other than the street, Louisville requires doors and windows also to appear on the primary street. Moreover, a building located on a corner must have either entrances on both streets or a corner entrance. This same provision of Louisville's code also encourages buildings to create a sense of enclosure by forming a *street wall*, bringing in another element of pedestrian-friendly design.

FORT WORTH, TEXAS
Near South Side Development Standards

Primary pedestrian building entrances shall be located on the street frontage of the building. For buildings fronting other public spaces, the primary pedestrian entrance shall be oriented to and accessible from the public space.

Fort Worth, Tex., Near Southside Dev. Standards and Guidelines § 5.C(3) (2008) (adopted as part of the city code by Fort Worth, Tex., Code appendix A, ch.4, § 4.909(D) (2009)).

Primary entrances should be oriented to a public sidewalk (Fort Worth, Texas).

LOUISVILLE, KENTUCKY | LAND DEVELOPMENT CODE
Building Location and Orientation

A. Principal building entrances shall face the primary street serving the development or shall be oriented toward a focal point such as a landscaped public square, plaza or similar formal public open space. All structures that are located along the primary street serving the development shall also have doors or windows facing the primary street (see B., below for lots with more than one street frontage). Principal buildings shall be parallel to the primary street. If the prevalent (more than 50%) orientation of buildings on the block is at an angle to the street, the new building's orientation shall be the same as other buildings. The walls of buildings on corners should be parallel to the streets.

B. Retail and office uses within buildings facing two or more streets shall have at least one customer entrance facing the primary street and one customer entrance facing the second street or instead of two entrances, a corner entrance.

Louisville, Ky., Land Dev. Code § 5.5.1 (A)(1) (2009).

Comfortable and Safe Places to Wait

BUS STOPS AND TRANSIT STATIONS PROVIDE THE PRIMARY INTERFACE between transit patrons and the transit system. For many potential transit users, the choice of whether or not to use transit is based, to a significant degree, on the quality of the wait experience at a stop or station.

The wait at a stop or station is just one of a series of sequential experiences in a typical transit trip. The other experiences include (1) the walk or drive from the trip origin to the transit stop; (2) the time spent on the bus or train; (3) if a transfer is required, the time waiting for the connecting bus or train; and (4) the walk to the final destination. Though these stages are obviously linked, passengers perceive the passage of time during each stage very differently. The time spent waiting is experienced as passing much more slowly (sometimes agonizingly so) than the time spent on the bus or train. Some studies estimate that wait time has a *disutility* effect that is seven times greater than the time spent actually moving in a vehicle (Pratt et al. 1999, p. 10-36). One must assume that conditions at a transit stop—principally comfort and safety—affect how onerous that wait time seems to transit users.

SEATING AND WEATHER PROTECTION

Comfort has two elements, seating and weather protection. Safety also has two, safety from crime and from traffic. Regarding comfort, protection from the elements can be provided by nearby buildings, when they are close to the street and designed with canopies, arcades, or other projections, which are standard fare in urban design and TOD manuals. Benches along the street are also commonly recommended, and both features serve pedestrians as well as transit users.

Where buildings are set back from the street, seating and weather protection must be provided via shelters, bus benches, and tree cover. In visual preference studies, having a shelter at a bus stop proved the most important determinant of bus stop selection and rating by transit users (Ewing 2000a). Shade from trees or building overhangs and the presence of a bench (absent a shelter) were also significant. These findings are consistent with other studies showing that transit riders are willing to walk farther to a bus stop if that stop is well sheltered (see, for example, Bodmer and Reiner 1977).

Public Space Amenities (Project for Public Spaces 2009), which provides design guidelines for bus shelters, specifies that the amount of seating at a shelter should be based on both the number of people who will use the shelter and the amount of time people will spend waiting. Where people wait for a long time, more seating is generally needed than at stops where the bus comes more frequently. Where there are large fluctuations between peak and off-peak use, a bus shelter can be designed with leaning rails, overhangs, and seating areas outside the shelter to accommodate the overflow.

Bus stops in some cities are spaced close together, often as close as every city block. This arrangement may preclude having shelters or benches at every stop. The TOD manual for Orlando, Florida, distinguishes between regular local stops and primary local stops, with the latter being equipped with shelters, benches, and fare and schedule information. Under this system, if primary stops are located every quarter to half mile along a route, most users will have access to a sheltered stop if they are willing to walk two or three extra minutes.

Transit stop with seating and shelter (Eugene, Oregon). | *Dan Burden*

LEFT: **Adequate shelter and transparency for natural surveillance (Cleveland, Ohio);** ABOVE: **Bus bulb (Miami Beach, Florida).** | *Sasaki; Reid Ewing*

SAFETY FROM CRIME AND TRAFFIC

The field of crime prevention through environmental design emphasizes natural surveillance, also called *eyes on the street*. This safeguard can be achieved with effective streetlighting and an open type of shelter design that will facilitate clear visibility from travel lanes and nearby buildings. Together, these measures ensure an ample supply of eyes on the street and can contribute to lower crime rates (Liggett, Loukaitou-Sideris, and Iseki 2001; Loukaitou-Sideris et al. 2001).

Equally important is safety from vehicle traffic. The two most effective features for protecting waiting transit riders from moving vehicles are a vertical curb and a setback from the street edge. These two measures provide psychological as well as physical protection, and both are highly ranked in visual preference literature.

Many TOD manuals recommend setting bus shelters and benches back from the street at least five feet. Although a good default value, a five-foot setback is not always feasible in urban settings, and it may be unnecessary if traffic speeds and volumes are moderate and streets have vertical curbs. Conversely, in suburban settings, with high design speeds and curbless profiles, a five-foot setback may not be enough to give transit users a sense of security.

Bus stops on main streets are ordinarily accommodated from the curbside lane rather than separate bus bays. On streets with curbside parking, the No Parking Zone at the nearside or farside of the intersection (or occasionally at midblock) serves as the bus pullout and boarding area. A few cities are experimenting with *bus bulbs*—curb extensions specifically designed to accommodate transit. They usually extend from the curb of the parking lane outward six feet, with the extra foot or two of parking lane affording a clear zone for cyclists.

With bus bulbs, buses stop to board passengers while in the travel lane instead of weaving into the parking lane and then having to merge back into traffic. Bus bulbs provide space for benches and shelters without crowding sidewalks or disrupting pedestrian flows. An evaluation of bus bulbs found that vehicle queues forming behind stopped buses—the main disadvantage of bus bulbs—were generally short and traffic delays comparable to conventional bus operations (Fitzpatrick et al. 2001).

A final safety-related consideration is whether to place bus stops on the nearside of an intersection, immediately before the intersection, or on the farside of the intersection, immediately after the intersection. Although each has advantages, and decisions should be made on a case-by-case basis, moving the stop to the farside tends to increase pedestrian safety. Alighting passengers and pedestrians are encouraged to cross behind the bus, at the farside crosswalk, rather than in front of the bus, at the nearside crosswalk. Pedestrians are therefore more visible to passing motorists (Texas Transportation Institute 1996).

The features highlighted in this chapter are the core, *must-have* elements for creating high-quality pedestrian environments. Their importance has long been demonstrated by a wide range of research and planning experience. It is understood that not all the elements will necessarily be achievable, especially in the normal political environment that surrounds most planning and development activities. Some, like small- to medium-sized blocks, might be particularly difficult to retrofit into existing built environments. We nevertheless emphasize these elements to help practitioners prioritize their efforts and to provide some assurance that their hard work will pay off.

Waiting Spaces

The following two codes creatively use the development process to increase the number and quality of public plazas and waiting spaces. Portland, Oregon's code innovatively allows the substitution of transit plazas for parking that would otherwise be required, encouraging attractive transit stops with more public space. Such transit plazas must be open to the public, and easements must be recorded to ensure that they remain so. The plazas must include seating, shelter, and landscaping. The code not only applies to new development; it also allows existing parking to be converted to transit plazas.

Salt Lake City's code takes a different approach, requiring developers to provide public space in proportion to the total floor area of the development. The code allows a choice of elements for the public space that will *activate* the space, including seating, trees, water features, and eating areas. Because use of outdoor space increases when there is a mixture of sun and shade, the option to include shade and trees increases the attractiveness of the space.

PORTLAND, OREGON | ZONING CODE

Main Street Node Overlay Code

Substitution of transit-supportive plazas for required parking. Sites where at least 20 parking spaces are required, and where at least one street lot line abuts a transit street may substitute transit-supportive plazas for required parking, as follows. Existing parking areas may be converted to take advantage of these provisions. Adjustments to the regulations of this paragraph are prohibited.

A. Transit-supportive plazas may be substituted for up to 10 percent of the required parking spaces on the site;

B. The plaza must be adjacent to and visible from the transit street. If there is a bus stop along the site's frontage, the plaza must be adjacent to the bus stop;

C. The plaza must be at least 300 square feet in area and be shaped so that a 10'×10' square will fit entirely in the plaza; and

D. The plaza must include all of the following elements:
  (1) A plaza open to the public. The owner must record a public access easement that allows public access to the plaza;
  (2) A bench or other sitting area with at least 5 linear feet of seating;
  (3) A shelter or other weather protection. The shelter must cover at least 20 square feet. If the plaza is adjacent to the bus stop, TriMet must approve the shelter; and
  (4) Landscaping. At least 10 percent, but not more than 25 percent of the transit-supportive plaza must be landscaped to the L1 standard of Chapter 33.248, Landscaping and Screening. This landscaping is in addition to any other landscaping or screening required for parking areas by the Zoning Code.

Portland, Ore., Code § 33.266.110(B)(5) (2009).

SALT LAKE CITY, UTAH

Zoning Code

Public spaces shall be provided as follows:

A. One square foot of plaza, park, or public space shall be required for every ten (10) square feet of gross building floor area.

B. Plazas or public spaces shall incorporate at least three (3) of the five (5) following elements:

  (1) Sitting space of at least one sitting space for each two hundred fifty (250) square feet shall be included in the plaza. Seating shall be a minimum of sixteen inches (16") in height and thirty inches (30") in width. Ledge benches shall have a minimum depth of thirty inches (30");
  (2) A mixture of areas that provide shade;
  (3) Trees in proportion to the space at a minimum of one tree per eight hundred (800) square feet, at least two inch (2") caliper when planted;
  (4) Water features or public art; and/or
  (5) Outdoor eating areas or food vendors.

Salt Lake City, Utah, Code § 21A.59.060(M)(2) (2009).

CHAPTER 4

CHECKLIST
of Highly Desirable Features

- Supportive commercial uses
- Grid-like street networks
- Traffic calming
- Closely spaced shade trees
- Little dead space
- Nearby parks and other public spaces
- Small-scale buildings (or articulated larger ones)
- Pedestrian-scale lighting
- Attractive transit facilities

This chapter presents the second checklist of design features, focusing on those that are highly desirable but not essential for creating environments conducive to pedestrian activity and transit use.

Supportive Commercial Uses

TOD MANUALS SOMETIMES SEEK TO CLASSIFY LAND USES as either inherently auto oriented or potentially transit oriented. Once classified, the idea is to channel the transit-oriented uses into the areas around transit stops and stations, while restricting the auto-oriented uses to areas that cannot be efficiently served by transit. It is a good idea, as far as it goes. In our main-street visual preference survey (Ewing et al. 2005), traditional shopping streets tended to get higher ratings than streets with a preponderance of residential development and other uses.

Examples of transit- and auto-oriented land uses, from three TOD manuals, are presented in figure 4-1. Although anomalies and inconsistencies that appeared on such lists were once commonplace, the three lists presented in the figure illustrate an emerging consensus about what types of land uses are transit supportive and what types are not.

Perhaps a better way to distinguish between auto- and transit-oriented uses is on the basis of performance standards, which directly relate the goal of creating successful transit- and pedestrian-oriented areas with the characteristics necessary to achieve that goal. For example, the uses generally considered excessively auto oriented, such as manufacturing and certain big-box stores,

Transit-oriented commercial uses (Vancouver, British Columbia). | *Dan Burden*

tend to fall toward the lower end of the range for "employees per 1,000 square feet of gross floor area" (see figure 4-2).

Other performance standards that could be used in addition to, or in place of, employee/space ratios are floor/area ratios (FARs), building lot coverage, or setback measures. By focusing on functional outcomes and quantifiable measures, even nominally auto-oriented uses can adapt to become transit supportive. Conversely, if standards are not met, even nominally transit-oriented uses should be restricted to locations that are not as well served by transit. This approach seems more reasonable and defensible than a blanket exclusion of certain land uses and blanket inclusion of others near station areas.

This performance-based approach was introduced in the Netherlands in the early 1990s through a planning policy known as the *right business in the right place*, or more familiarly the *ABC policy* (Bartholomew 1995). Under the policy, cities classify urban locations according to their accessibility profiles: *A* locations have superior access to public transit; *B* locations have good access to both transit and highways; *C* locations have superior access to highways; and *R* locations do not have good access to either mode. When a business proposes the construction of a new facility, the company is assessed according to its mobility profile, which accounts for the density of workers and visitors, the mobility needs of employees (to accomplish their jobs, not to commute), and the need to transport goods. The mobility profile of the business is then matched with a location having a suitable accessibility profile. Businesses with high employer or visitor densities and few requirements for employee mobility and freight transportation are directed to A locations;

FIGURE 4-1

Transit- and Auto-Oriented Land Uses from Three TOD Manuals

Manual	Potentially Transit Oriented	Inherently Auto Oriented
City of Ottawa, Ontario, *Transit-Oriented Development Guidelines* (2007)	Townhouses; apartments; child care facilities; hotels; medical clinics; restaurants; affordable housing; libraries; recreational and cultural facilities; fitness clubs; movie theaters; call centers; offices; high schools; postsecondary institutions	Automotive parts, repair, and service; car dealerships; car washes; drive-through facilities; gas/service stations; commercial surface parking; warehouse storage; animal boarding; commercial nurseries; low-density residential developments on large lots
City of Austin, Texas, *Transit-Oriented Development Guidebook* (2006)	Multifamily and small-lot single-family residential; offices; hotels; health care facilities; medical clinics; high schools and colleges; daycare facilities; cultural institutions; athletic/recreational facilities; health clubs; personal services; retail shops; restaurants; grocery stores; coffee shops; local pubs; outdoor cafés; entertainment facilities; neighborhood-oriented businesses; financial institutions; dry cleaners	Automotive sales; car washes; large-format food stores; warehouse distribution; regional parks; large-format faith facilities; low-density single-family residential; automotive services and repair; large-format/warehouse retail; drive-in/drive-through services; outdoor storage; funeral homes; parking lots; low-intensity industrial uses
Capital Area Transportation Authority, *Designing for Transit-Oriented Development in Greater Lansing* (2011)	Multidwelling residential; affordable housing; retail shops; grocery stores; restaurants; offices; hotels; health care facilities; medical clinics; high schools and colleges; daycare facilities; cultural institutions; athletic/recreational facilities; health clubs; entertainment facilities	Parking lots; warehouses; automotive services; car washes; warehouse distribution; regional parks; storage facilities; low-density housing; low-intensity industrial uses; gas stations; strip malls; areas with poor walkability

FIGURE 4-2

Employee Space Requirements of Different Land Uses

Land Use	Employees/1,000 Ft² Gross Floor Area
Sit-down restaurant	9.92 (1993)
Medical-dental office building	4.05
Government office building	3.60
Bank (drive-through)	3.50
General office building	3.20
Hospital	3.17
Daycare center	2.82
Discount store	1.98
Manufacturing plant	1.79
New car sales	1.58
Hardware store	0.96
Furniture store	0.42

Source: ITE 2008.

those with low densities and numerous mobility and freight needs are directed to C locations; and those with intermediate mobility values are directed to B locations.

Regardless of the classification system used, the overall objective is to differentiate commercial development that is truly oriented toward transit from that which is merely adjacent to transit. The former is scaled, oriented, and of a type that is intended to attract transit users (though often not exclusively), whereas the latter is more or less oblivious to transit's presence. By nature and design, the latter is oriented toward car-driven customers; transit's proximity is coincidental. According to Cervero, Ferrell, and Murphy (2002, p. 6), transit-adjacent development is distinct from transit-oriented development because, although it is proximate to transit, it "fails to capitalize upon this proximity.... It lacks any functional connectivity to transit—whether in terms of land-use composition, means of station access, or site design."

Many auto-oriented land uses, however, can be tamed through clever site planning and building design. Many examples exist of fast-food restaurants and convenience stores that blend into traditional main-street settings. Small setbacks, on-street or rear parking, wall-mounted signs, and compatible architecture make them almost indistinguishable from neighboring shops. A publication by the American Planning Association and the Townscape Institute contains dozens of examples of how community design review can require corporate franchises to modify their appearance to respect or enhance community character (Fleming 2002).

Other auto-oriented uses—discount department stores, warehouse clubs, and home improvement centers—have building masses and parking requirements that are harder, but not impossible, to work with. By enacting design standards, such as making big-box retailers part of centers rather than strips, limiting floor areas, adding doors and windows to facades, making the architecture less boxy, building vertically rather than horizontally, and breaking up parking areas with small-pad commercial uses and landscaping, communities have made these stores more pedestrian oriented.

The most common way to tame big-box development is through limits on the size of stores. In Walpole, New Hampshire, stores are capped at 52,000 square feet; whereas in Coconino County, Arizona, retail stores are limited to 70,000 square feet. Another promising approach is to limit the footprint of stores. Gaithersburg, Maryland's ordinance allows larger stores but limits their footprint to 80,000 square feet, which has resulted in several two-story big-box buildings (Beaumont and Tucker 2002). Traditional big-box retailers such as Target and Walmart are responding to these initiatives, adapting

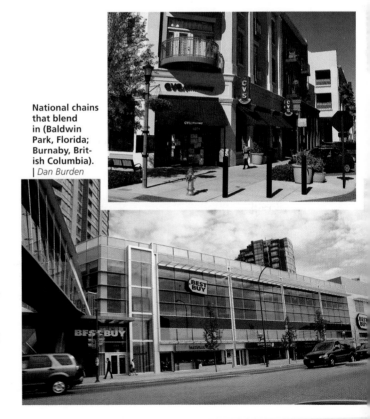

National chains that blend in (Baldwin Park, Florida; Burnaby, British Columbia).
| Dan Burden

their normal large footprint and horizontal floor plans to produce more vertical, smaller outlets. Probably one of the most dramatic examples of this trend is Target's recent move into Louis Sullivan's historic Carson Pirie Scott Building in downtown Chicago. Walmart, meanwhile, is constructing an 80,000-square-foot store in a multi-

story building at a new Metro station in Tysons Corner, Virginia, with underground parking and other uses above the store.

Comprehensive design standards are even more effective in taming big-box stores. Moscow, Idaho, requires all "large retail establishments" (that is, those larger than

LOCAL CODE EXAMPLES
Supportive Commercial Uses

The codes for San Francisco and Seattle require commercial uses of the types that support pedestrian activity. San Francisco's code takes a similar but more detailed approach, explicitly noting the goal of supporting pedestrian-oriented commercial uses and laying out in detail the acceptable uses for street-level frontages on given streets. San Francisco also specifies that such uses shall not include uses oriented toward motor vehicles. Seattle's code takes a streamlined approach and requires that all lots on designated pedestrian-oriented streets have at street level a park, library, or supportive commercial use, such as a store, restaurant, or entertainment venue.

SAN FRANCISCO, CALIFORNIA
Planning Code

SEC. 145.4 REQUIRED GROUND FLOOR COMMERCIAL USES

(A) PURPOSE: To support active, pedestrian-oriented commercial uses on important commercial streets.

(B) APPLICABILITY [sets forth streets to which requirement applies].

(C) DEFINITIONS.

"Active commercial uses" shall include those uses specifically identified below in Table 145.4 [including amusement game arcade, animal hospital, automobile sale or rental (with qualifications), bar, business goods and equipment sales and repair service, eating and drinking use, entertainment, tourist-oriented gift store, institutions, jewelry store, neighborhood serving business, nonauto vehicle sales or rental (see qualification, above), public use (with qualifications), restaurant, retail sales and service, financial service, medical service, personal service, takeout food, trade shop, walk-up facility], and:

(1) Shall not include uses oriented to motor vehicles except for automobile sale or rental where curb-cuts, garage doors, or loading access are not utilized or proposed, and such sales or rental activity is entirely within an enclosed building and does not encroach on surrounding sidewalks or open spaces;

(2) Shall include public uses except for utility installations; and

(3) Shall not include residential care uses as defined in Sections 790.50, 790.51, and 890.50. . . .

(D) CONTROLS.

(1) Active commercial uses which are permitted by the specific district in which they are located are required on the ground floor of all street frontages listed in Subsection (b) above.

San Francisco, Cal., Plan. Code § 154.4 (2009).

SEATTLE, WASHINGTON
Land Use Code

STREET-LEVEL USES. One or more of the uses listed in subsection A are required at street level on all lots abutting streets designated as Class 1 Pedestrian Streets shown on Map B, located at the end of this Chapter. . . .

A. The following uses qualify as required street level uses:

　　1. General sales and service uses;

　　2. Eating and drinking establishments;

　　3. Entertainment uses;

　　4. Public libraries; and

　　5. Public parks.

Seattle, Wash., Mun. Code § 23.48.019(A) (2009).

Street-level retail uses (Seattle, Washington). | *Adrienne Schmitz*

40,000 square feet) to vary facade depths; to provide windows, entrances, or awnings for at least 60 percent of the facade width; to locate entrances on at least two building sides; to design entrances to include porticos, arcades, and corniced parapets; and to incorporate variations in material color, texture, or type every 30 feet of facade width (City of Moscow 2010). This requirement is on top of the city's prohibition of large retail establishments in the central business and urban mixed commercial districts. Portland, Oregon, which generally requires all new or renovated retail buildings to be adjacent to and oriented toward public streets, provides an exception for big-box stores (100,000 square feet or larger) that allows them to be located back from the street if the parking lot is broken into virtual blocks by lanes designed to emulate local streets. The lanes must include curbs, sidewalks, street trees, even the simulation of on-street parking (City of Portland 2009).

Grid-Like Street Networks

AT LEAST SINCE THE EARLY 1960S, planners have been on a quest for street networks that combine the mobility of the grid with the safety and topographic sensitivity of curvilinear streets. Christopher Tunnard and Boris Pushkarev (1963, p. 98), in their classic *Man-Made America: Chaos or Control?*, argue that hybrid street networks can have an order to them that is easily perceived by travelers, but an order that is not simple, mechanistic, and monotonous like that of a standard grid. It is a complex order ("variety within unity," as they put it) that affords the best possible aesthetics. Even before Tunnard and Pushkarev, Kevin Lynch (1960) spoke of modifications to the rectangular grid that would overcome its visual monotony, disregard for topography, vulnerability to through-traffic, and lack of differentiation between heavily traveled and lightly traveled ways.

The traditional street grid has several advantages from a traffic engineering standpoint. Traffic is dispersed rather than concentrated; alternative routes are available whenever one route becomes unusually clogged; the need for traffic signals, and resulting interruptions in traffic flow, are held to a minimum by the many left-turn opportunities available in a grid. Because of the increased directness of travel, the grid can also result in reduced vehicle travel (Litman 2011). In one study, gridded street patterns account for a 43 percent reduction in vehicle miles traveled compared with a conventional suburban street pattern (Proft and Condon 2001).

The traditional grid has several advantages for pedestrians as well. It offers relatively direct routes compared with contemporary networks with curving streets and culs-de-sac. It offers alternatives to travel along high-volume routes, since parallel streets always exist in a grid (Marshall and Garrick 2010). It is legible—that is, it gives pedestrians a clear sense of orientation. It has contextual continuity—that is, it gives pedestrians a sense of orderly progression from place to place.

The grid also has real estate and development advantages. By some reports, a rectilinear street pattern can reduce developer costs for road infrastructure by as much as 40 percent compared with conventional suburban patterns (Steuteville 2009).

The traditional grid is actively promoted in many TOD manuals. It allows transit vehicles to avoid backtracking

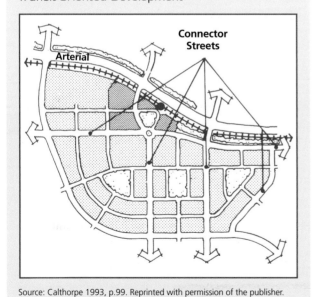

FIGURE 4-3

Orderly Pattern of Connector Streets within a Transit-Oriented Development

Source: Calthorpe 1993, p.99. Reprinted with permission of the publisher.

FIGURE 4-4

Hybrid Network with Connectivity Index of 1.53 (Orenco Station, Oregon)

Source: ESRI Imagery.

FIGURE 4-5

Hybrid Network with Connectivity Index of 1.50 (Southern Village, North Carolina)

Source: ESRI Imagery.

and frequent turns, and it offers transit users more direct access to transit stops.

The grid also has disadvantages, mainly related to safety and topographic sensitivity. Topographic sensitivity is an obvious problem, especially when one considers places like San Francisco, where a rigid rectangular grid overlays the land with almost no regard to a widely varying topography. Safety problems are also reported in the literature. Injury severity in pedestrian and bicycle crashes tends to be greater on gridded streets without traffic calming, compared with neighborhoods with "loop-and-lollipop" street patterns (Rifaat, Tay, and de Barros 2011). Yet it depends on the nature of intersections (four-way versus three-way) and spacing between them (long blocks versus short blocks). "Generalizing, it appears that the shorter the uninterrupted length of roadway, the slower the traffic will travel and the less severe any crashes will be. Short stretches ending in T-intersections are particularly effective in reducing speed, crash frequency, and crash severity" (Ewing and Dumbaugh 2009, p. 354).

Grid-like street networks often go hand in hand with another essential feature, short blocks. The two features are conceptually distinct though. That is, networks can be more or less grid-like with shorter or longer blocks. A supergrid of arterials at mile section lines is grid-like, but it does not meet the short block test. Likewise, a curvilinear street network with short blocks does not meet the grid-like test. Of the two features, short blocks would appear to be the more important based on their relationship to walking and transit use and the frequency with which they are regulated (Handy, Paterson, and Butler 2003). Hence, grid-like street networks are categorized as highly desirable rather than essential.

Looking at all the evidence, *Best Development Practices* (Ewing 1996) recommends hybrid networks and introduces an index with which to measure street connectivity along a continuum between the traditional urban grid, such as Midtown Manhattan, and the contemporary suburban network, like Reston, Virginia. This connectivity index, computed by dividing the number of links in the network by the number of nodes, has been adopted in land development codes, such as Orlando, Florida's and the state of Virginia's subdivision street standards. Hybrid networks typically have index values in the range of 1.4 to 1.6, considerably higher than much of suburbia but lower than traditional cities and towns. Street networks of new urbanist communities often fall within this range (see figures 4-4 and 4-5).

Grid-Like Street Networks

San Diego's code calls for a grid pattern explicitly. It also allows a modified grid, providing flexibility that may enable it to maximize the benefits of a grid while avoiding some of the drawbacks, particularly in places where topography makes a grid less practical. The code provides for short blocks and recognizes pedestrians' desire to reach destinations without crossing busy streets. The code also calls for streets to frame vistas to enhance visual interest and orientation for pedestrians. St. Lucie County, Florida's code provides for an interconnected network but puts less emphasis on a grid per se, allowing streets to be curved or bent as long as they connect to other streets. St. Lucie emphasizes short routes and connectivity between attractive pedestrian destinations, such as schools, parks, and retail. Interestingly, both San Diego and St. Lucie call for alleys as one method of balancing vehicle and pedestrian needs.

SAN DIEGO, CALIFORNIA | MUNICIPAL CODE
Urban Village Overlay Zone

STREET PATTERN. The layout of the street system shall be in a grid pattern or modified grid pattern, emphasizing interconnected streets and the ability to reach local destinations without crossing major streets or primary arterials. It is desirable to have streets with block faces of 400 feet in length or less. The use of alleys is encouraged. Where possible, streets should frame vistas of the mixed-use core, public buildings, parks, and natural features.

San Diego, Cal., Mun. Code § 132.1109(a) (2009).

ST. LUCIE COUNTY, FLORIDA
Land Development Regulations

Each neighborhood must provide an interconnected network of streets, alleys or lanes, and other public passageways.

I. Neighborhood streets must be designed to encourage pedestrian and bicycle travel by providing short routes to connect residential uses with nearby commercial services, schools, parks, and other neighborhood facilities within the same or adjoining Towns or Villages. Sidewalks and rows of street trees must be provided on both sides of all neighborhood streets. . . .

III. Neighborhood streets do not have to form an orthogonal grid and are not required to intersect at ninety-degree angles. These streets may be curved or bent but must connect to other streets. . . .

VII. A continuous network of rear and side alleys and/or lanes is desirable to serve as the primary means of vehicular ingress to individual lots.

St. Lucie County, Fla., Land Dev. Code ch. 3, § 3.01.03.EE.2.k(2) (2009).

Traffic Calming

MANY U.S. COMMUNITIES HAVE ARTERIALS AND COLLECTORS with fronting residential or commercial properties. They may be old rural highways overtaken by development; neighborhood streets at the end of a tributary network; through-streets with fronting residences that have attracted growing volumes of cut-through traffic; or main streets that have become speedways. Whether by design or as a result of growth, thousands of vehicles per day race past homes, shops, schools, and parks.

The pedestrian environment suffers greatly as traffic volumes and speeds pass certain thresholds. A line of parked cars can act as a buffer, as can a row of street trees or streetlights. If nothing else, sidewalks can be set back some distance from the street. But even with a buffer, no sidewalk will be inviting to pedestrians if it sits next to a high-speed, high-volume thoroughfare,

hence the desirability of traffic calming on access routes to transit stops, commercial centers, schools and parks, and other trip attractors.

Traffic calming is becoming a mainstream activity of the transportation field in the United States. There are now hundreds of local programs and several state initiatives. Some of the newer TOD manuals call for traffic-calming

FIGURE 4-6

Street Use Before and After Traffic Calming, Berkeley, California

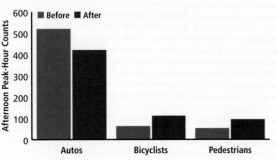

FIGURE 4-7

Street Use Before and After Traffic Calming, Vinderup, Denmark

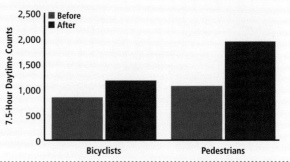

measures on access routes to transit stops. Hedonic price studies suggest that traffic calming may increase property values under certain circumstances, and public support in the United States for neighborhood-scale traffic-calming interventions is growing. A study in El Cajon, California, reported a 181 percent increase in property values and a 56 percent increase in leasing rates since traffic-calming measures were completed in 1996 (PBIC and APBP 2009).

There is also some evidence that traffic calming increases walking and bicycling. A study of street use before and after traffic calming on Milvia Street in Berkeley, California, found that pedestrian and bicycle traffic increased by almost 80 percent after traffic calming, whereas auto traffic declined by 20 percent (see figure 4-6). European studies suggest similar benefits (see figure 4-7) and point to significant reductions in vehicle crashes (Elvik 2001).

Thus, it is tempting to include traffic calming among the *essential* features of pedestrian- and transit-friendly environments. The authors hesitate only because relatively few streets in the United States, including many good ones, are presently traffic calmed.

U.S. traffic-calming practice is still in its formative stages, so European examples are offered for guidance. A detailed description of European practice can be found in *U.S. Traffic Calming Manual* (Ewing and Brown 2009b, chapter 6).

European programs are more oriented to the needs of pedestrians and bicyclists than U.S. programs. Europe calms main roads—what in the United States would be classified as arterials—as they penetrate communities, whereas traffic calming in the United States is mostly

limited to local streets, and residential streets at that. The problem, as one writer put it, is that "making 99 percent of a journey safe and convenient by foot or bike is futile if the remaining one percent contains a dangerous road crossing" (Tolley 1990, p. 73).

In the early 1980s, Norway needed a policy to deal with intercity traffic speeding through its many small towns. Because of budget constraints, the nation could not afford to build bypasses around all of them. The government decided its one viable option was traffic calming. Inspired by Norway, Denmark undertook a test of traffic-calming measures applied to highways through three small towns. Prewarnings or *gateways* were placed at the town entries, and *chicanes* (S-shaped street realignments), roundabouts, *chokers* (curb extensions), and other measures were installed in the town centers. The results included a drop in speeds, decline in accidents, and improvement in air quality, all at one-fourth to one-third the cost of constructing a bypass. This outcome led to a series of similar projects on main roads throughout Denmark.

These positive results helped encourage many cities across the globe to adopt area-wide traffic-calming programs. Notable examples include Odense in Denmark; Göteborg and Malmö in Sweden; Amsterdam, Delft, Gronignen, The Hague, and Tilburg in the Netherlands; Bologna and Parma in Italy; and Basel and Zurich in Switzerland. Some U.S. cities are beginning to calm arterials, and many already calm collectors (Ewing and Brown 2009a).

Another area where Europe leads the United States is in the use of pedestrian- and bicycle-friendly traffic-calming measures. In Europe, all of the following are

BELOW: **Speed cushions with wheel cutouts for emergency vehicles and bicycles (Sacramento, California); RIGHT: Raised crosswalk for traffic calming (Paris, France).** | *Reid Ewing*

common: center island narrowings with pedestrian crossings; chokers with bicycle bypass lanes; raised crosswalks and raised intersections for pedestrians; and provision of separate rights-of-way for cyclists with special bike turn lanes and traffic signals (Fischer et al. 2010). Some U.S. jurisdictions are beginning to follow suit. Albuquerque, New Mexico, and Howard County, Maryland, have examples of chokers with bicycle bypass lanes. Austin, Texas, and Sacramento, California, have begun to use speed cushions instead of speed humps in certain applications, in part because they view the cushions as more bicycle friendly. Bellevue, Washington, has made raised crosswalks a central part of its program, us-

ing them routinely at school crossings. Eugene, Oregon, has several raised intersections.

It is clearly more cost-effective to design streets for speed and volume control at the outset than to have to go back to fix traffic problems, as hundreds of U.S. communities are now doing. Built before the automobile, many European streets were sized for lower speeds. More recently, continental Europe, Britain, and Australia have adopted "skinny street" standards for new developments that are much narrower than the standard suburban design norms and are designed for equity of use among drivers, bicyclists, and pedestrians (Girling 2005).

The United States can follow Europe's lead when it comes to street standards as well as traffic-calming policies. New subdivision street standards were adopted by the Howard County Council in Maryland. The standards mandate narrower streets; require roundabouts at higher-volume, four-legged intersections; and provide for sharp bends and other slow points at regular intervals. In response to Oregon's Transportation Planning Rule, which strives to reduce reliance on the automobile, Eugene adopted the Eugene Local Street Plan. The plan

FIGURE 4-8

Narrow Residential Street Cross Section (Charlotte, North Carolina)

Development Zone | Pedestrian Zone | Green Zone | Mixed Vehicle and Parking Zone | Green Zone | Pedestrian Zone | Development Zone

5' | 8' | 2" | 2" | 8' | 5'

20' B.O.C. TO B.O.C.*

Source: Charlotte Department of Transportation 2007.

requires interconnectedness of local streets and replaces the city's old hierarchy of wide streets with a new hierarchy of narrower streets, starting with access lanes 21 feet wide and moving up to medium-volume residential streets that are 27 to 34 feet wide.

In late 2007, Charlotte, North Carolina, adopted new urban street design guidelines. They identify the multimodal purpose of each type of street in the hierarchy, including minimum service levels by mode for each street and intersection. For each type, guidelines are provided for the *development zone*, *pedestrian zone*, *green zone*, and *vehicle and parking zone*. For local residential streets, the intent is to keep the paved area as narrow as possible. Three street widths are specified (all measured from back of curb to back of curb):

- **NARROW (20 FEET)**—to be used when parking is expected to be light and limited to one side of the street at a given location;
- **MEDIUM (27 FEET)**—to be used as the default; and
- **WIDE (35 FEET)**—to be used when parking is expected to be heavy on both sides of the street.

In addition to encouraging narrow streets, Charlotte's guidelines also specify the use of traffic calming on local streets, with an objective of slow points every 300 to 500 feet.

The main impediment to traffic-calmed streets in the United States is resistance from fire and emergency medical services. Ewing, Stevens, and Brown (2007) give examples of creative design solutions negotiated between developers and service providers, such as alleys, sprinklers, parking on only one side, wider turning radii,

LOCAL CODE EXAMPLES

Traffic Calming

San Antonio, Texas's code acknowledges that street design can lead to excessive speeds and provides for various traffic-calming devices, such as bulbouts, roundabouts, and median islands. The code permits longer streets where there are traffic-calming features. In Bloomington, Indiana, a neighborhood traffic safety program developed by the city engineering department and the bicycle and pedestrian safety commission determined appropriate locations and types of traffic-calming devices in neighborhoods. The Bloomington code simply sets out where the traffic-calming features would be installed and specifies whether they will be speed tables, speed humps, traffic islands, traffic circles, street narrowing, bulbouts, or intersection realignment.

SAN ANTONIO, TEXAS
Unified Development Code

TRAFFIC CALMING. The purpose of this section, is to protect the public health, safety and general welfare by ensuring that speeds on local streets are suitable for their intended purpose. The city hereby finds and determines that long blocks, wide street cross sections and uninterrupted traffic flows can encourage speeding on local streets. Accordingly, these design standards will slow traffic on local streets while allowing flexibility in design and offering applicants the choice of treatment that works best for the streets in a proposed development.

(1) APPLICABILITY. The provisions of this subsection shall apply to local streets when any traffic control devices are proposed and shall be approved by both the city and the county when located in the ETJ [Extraterritorial Jurisdiction].

(2) STREET LENGTHS. The length of street links shall comply with the block length standards established in subsection 35-515(b)(3) of this chapter.

(3) TRAFFIC CONTROL CALMING FEATURES. A longer street length may be allowed through the placement of an approved traffic calming feature at a location which produces an unimpeded length of the street link which does not exceed the block length standards (subsection 35-515(b)(4)).

Table 506-8 provisions describe and establish standards for permitted traffic calming devices [such as bulbouts, roundabouts, speed humps, median islands, T-intersections] where traffic calming measures are permitted as part of the roadway design elements in subsection B, above.

San Antonio, Tex., Unified Dev. Code art. V, div. 2, § 35-506(t) (2009).

BLOOMINGTON, INDIANA
Municipal Code

Traffic calming locations. The locations described in Schedule J-1 shall have devices installed for the purpose of neighborhood traffic calming.

Bloomington, Ind., Mun. Code § 15.26.040 (2009).

and load-bearing pavers on corners. One of the most promising options is the use of speed cushions, raised, rounded areas placed laterally across a road surface with gaps strategically designed to accommodate the wider wheel widths of emergency vehicles; passenger vehicles, with their narrower wheel bases, still hit the cushions and hence are encouraged to drive slowly. The streets so designed are narrow enough to control speeds without additional traffic-calming measures.

Note that European traffic calming does not preclude high-volume, high-speed thoroughfares linking different communities and districts within urban areas. It simply ensures that within communities and districts, streets will act as a unifying rather than dividing force. Or put another way, *roads* are fine elsewhere, but within communities and districts, all public ways should be designed to function as *streets* with all that term implies.

Closely Spaced Shade Trees

IF THE APPROPRIATE TREES ARE PLANTED IN THE RIGHT LOCATIONS with the proper spacing, they contribute to nearly all pedestrian-oriented design qualities (see chapter 2). In a world of isolated bits and pieces, there is a hunger for order. Street trees can provide it. And trees can hide a multitude of architectural sins. The memorable quality of cities like Savannah, old Philadelphia, and Paris is as much due to organized patterns of trees as architecture and urban design (Arnold 1993, p. 2).

A widely accepted view is that street trees provide shade, privacy, better aesthetics, and a sense of safety for pedestrians by buffering them from vehicular traffic. The increased sense of pedestrian safety may be why street trees are a factor in determining whether children walk or bike to school (Larsen et al. 2009). It is also probably one of the reasons why street trees prove so important in visual preference studies. In our study of bus stops, trees along streets leading to bus stops were the second most highly valued feature (Ewing 2000a). Likewise, in our study of main streets, the proportion of

street frontage covered by tree canopy was the second most valued feature (Ewing et al. 2006).

Mature shade trees have been shown to provide economic benefits to communities (Millward and Sabir 2011; Soares et al. 2011). A hedonic price study by the Portland Bureau of Planning and Sustainability showed that street trees add 6.4 percent to the mean sales price of a home, as well as increase the value of nearby homes. The combined effects of the number of trees fronting a property and the tree crown area within 100 feet of a house can add more than $8,000 to the price

Memorable pedestrian environments (Bilbao, Spain; Philadelphia, Pennsylvania). | *Adrienne Schmitz*

LEFT: **Outdoor room created with shade trees (San Jose, California); BELOW: Trees mediate the scale of high-rise buildings (Chicago, Illinois).** | *Reid Ewing; VHT Photography*

of a house, "the equivalent of adding 129 finished square feet to its floor plan" (Donovan and Butry 2010; White 2009, p. 28).

It is tempting to label closely spaced shade trees an essential feature of pedestrian- and transit-oriented streets, particularly in the southern United States with its high temperatures and high humidity. On a bioclimatic chart for a place like Miami, the combination of temperature and humidity for most of the year puts it above the "shading line," where shade is always required, and wind protection often required, for outdoor comfort (Brown 1985).

Yet as with traffic calming, it seems unreasonable to label any feature *essential* that is in such short supply. This reasoning applies doubly to central cities, the areas considered most pedestrian and transit oriented. With regard to tree cover, many cities are more deficient than suburbs, which themselves are often terribly deficient (Arnold 1993, p. 7).

Size, location, and spacing all become critical variables in street tree planting. Generally speaking, shade trees that will reach a height of 50–70 feet at maturity and have a canopy starting at a comfortable 15 feet or so above the ground make the best street trees. The constant movement of branches and leaves, and the ever-changing patterns of light created, add to the visual complexity of the streetscape. The low canopy contrasts with the monumentality of tall buildings and wide spaces, creating human scale within larger volumes.

The ideal location for street trees is between the street and sidewalk (see chapter 3, "Appropriate Buffering from Traffic"). Trees planted between the street and sidewalk provide a physical and psychological barrier between large-mass vehicles and small-mass pedestrians. In this location, trees visually enclose street space; they extend pedestrian space from buildings to the street; and they shade the entire right-of-way, both street and sidewalk.

The best spacing of trees places them close enough together to form a continuous canopy over the sidewalk and a buffer between the street and sidewalk. This arrangement requires spacing of 30 feet or less center to center, not the 50-70 feet typically called for in land development codes. When trees are first planted, they must be close together to define street space at all. As they mature over decades, closely spaced trees will have higher, more translucent canopies that produce an uninterrupted quality of light and shade.

Streets cited as outstanding examples in Henry Arnold's (1993, pp. 173–81) extraordinarily insightful *Trees in Urban Design* nearly all have street trees no more than 30 feet apart. Likewise, Allan Jacobs (1993) finds, after painstaking measurements of the distances between trees on innumerable streets, that they should be planted at a distance of between 15 and 25 feet apart in a continuous line. Wherever possible, it is important that no breaks occur in the line for building entrances, bus stops, or curb cuts. Even the safety standard of 40–50 feet between trees and street corners is not exempt from Jacobs's ire: "If trees are dangerous, then why is a light pole or traffic signal pole with a diameter larger than a redwood and with a large electronic box attached to it permitted at the corner?" (1993, p. 84). He turns to successful examples, such as Viale Manlio Gelsomini in Rome and Pennsylvania Avenue in Washing-

ton, D.C., to illustrate the importance of continuous tree lines on well-designed streets. Dumbaugh's (2006a) safety analysis of roadside design supports Jacobs's assertions.

The standard suburban practice is just the opposite of what is recommended above. Small ornamental and flowering trees, fruit trees, palms, and evergreens usually substitute for substantial shade trees. They are placed far apart and often set on the farside of the sidewalk close to the right-of-way line, where they pose less risk to errant vehicles but fail to serve most purposes. It is a perverse world, indeed, where errant vehicles are afforded more protection from trees than pedestrians are from errant vehicles. Used in these ways, trees may decorate a street or hide an unpleasant view, but they contribute little to the fundamentals of good design—qualities such as visual enclosure.

LOCAL CODE EXAMPLES

Street Trees

Both Arlington, Virginia, and Peoria, Illinois, require street trees to be spaced at an average of not more than 30 feet apart, a distance that meets street tree spacing recommendations. Arlington's code requires trees on every street within the design area. Arlington also requires a minimum amount of unpaved ground in order to promote the trees' health and requires trees to be a minimum size when planted. The Peoria code makes developers responsible for planting trees along the property that is being developed. Peoria allows some flexibility in the spacing of trees but prohibits spacing them more than 45 feet apart. In a related provision, Peoria requires a minimum unpaved area per tree and also requires the bare ground to be covered with a plant groundcover.

ARLINGTON, VIRGINIA

Zoning Ordinance

Each STREET shall have canopy shade trees (STREET TREES). Wherever the REGULATING PLAN does not show specific STREET TREE placement, STREET TREES shall be planted along the STREET TREE ALIGNMENT LINE at an average spacing not greater than 25 to 30 feet on center (measured per BLOCK face). Required tree planting area widths are specified on the typical street cross sections in the Master Transportation Plan—Part I. However, open soil surface area shall be not less than 60 square feet (with a minimum of 5 feet in any direction) per isolated tree, and connected (tree strip) planting areas are encouraged. The planting area's minimum dimension shall be not less than 5 feet. At planting, trees shall be at least 4 to 4.5 inches in diameter (4 feet above grade) and at least 12 feet in overall height. Species shall be selected from the Columbia Pike Special Revitalization District Street Tree List. Consult the ADMINISTRATIVE REVIEW TEAM for the designated tree species for a particular STREET.

Arlington County, Va., Zoning Ordinance § 20, app. A (V)(B) (2009).

PEORIA, ILLINOIS

Land Development Code

At the time of development, the applicant is responsible for installing/planting the following street trees in the space fronting their property between the required building line and the travel lane. . . . Each street-space shall have street trees planted along the street tree alignment line (generally three feet, six inches from the back of the curb) at an average spacing not greater than 30 feet on center (measured per block face). Required tree planting area widths are specified in the Street Type Specifications or on the regulating plan. Where necessary, spacing allowances may be made to accommodate curb cuts, fire hydrants and other infrastructure elements, however, at no location shall spacing exceed 45 feet on center.

Peoria, Ill., Code app. C, § 6.8.3(b) (2009).

On the subject of street trees and traffic safety, lateral clearance between trees and the curb face may be as small as one and a half feet and still meet the American Association of State Highway and Transportation Officials' "Green Book" guideline for low-speed streets with vertical curbs (AASHTO 2004b). The low speeds and straight alignments of main streets largely eliminate safety concerns associated with trees as fixed objects. Indeed, street trees and landscaping may actually improve the safety of urban streets (Ewing and Dumbaugh 2009).

Trees may be located in tree wells, planters, or planting strips, depending on the nature of the street. Larger planting beds are preferred for the sake of both trees and sidewalks. Where sidewalk width is lacking, trees may be placed on curb extensions.

Street trees are sometimes planted in medians of boulevards. A median width of six feet will provide more than sufficient lateral clearance to meet AASHTO minimum requirements and will afford even large trees plenty of space in which to grow. Trees planted within the median reduce the perceived width of streets and may calm traffic.

BELOW: **Street trees buffer pedestrian space and reduce drivers' psychological space (Beijing, China);** UPPER RIGHT: **Treed median reduces the perceived width of a street;** LOWER RIGHT: **Trees on curb extensions (Lake Oswego, Oregon).** | *Reid Ewing (below); Dan Burden (upper and lower right)*

Little Dead Space

DEAD SPACES INCLUDE PARKING LOTS (EMPTY OR FULL), LONG BLANK WALLS, VACANT LOTS, reflective-glass facades, earth berms so high that nothing is visible above them, featureless open spaces, and garage doors lined up along the street. What makes these spaces "dead" is the impression that no people are nearby.

The main problem with dead street frontage is that it renders streetscapes less complex, and hence less interesting to pedestrians (see chapter 2). The human eye can register about three objects per second (Untermann 1984, p. 16). Motorists moving as slowly as 20 miles per hour can take in only three features as they pass a 30-foot-wide building. The faster they go, the more *tunnel vision* sets in. Fine building and streetscape details are lost to high-speed motorists.

On the other hand, a pedestrian passing the same 30-foot-wide building at three miles per hour is capable of discerning some 20 details. Unlike the motorist, the pedestrian is free to look around, stop whenever he or she pleases, and focus on objects outside the right-of-way, making building and streetscape details extremely important if pedestrian interest is to be maintained (Gehl, Kaefer, and Reigstad 2006).

Of greatest interest to pedestrians are other people, whether on the street or visible off the street at home, work, or play. People and their movements add to the street imageability, complexity, human scale, and other urban design qualities (see chapter 2). Consumer goods in display windows and building interiors visible from the street rank high too. If nothing else draws attention, architectural details can engage the eye.

Designers promote active street-level land uses with such fervor that it came as a surprise when dead space proved a secondary influence on visual preference in our main-street visual preference study (Ewing et al. 2005). In the survey, the proportion of street frontage made up of dead spaces was a significant determinant of main-street scores but was less significant than other variables. In the urban design qualities survey, the proportion of active uses (the opposite of dead space) was a significant contributor to the rated transparency of streetscapes, but again it was less significant than other variables (Ewing and Handy 2009). Counted as dead spaces were vacant lots, public parking lots, private parking lots separating commercial buildings from the street, driveways interrupting the continuity of street frontage, and blank walls.

Given these findings, minimizing dead street frontage has been downgraded to the second tier of pedestrian- and transit-oriented features. It is important, but possibly less so for utilitarian trips than sometimes assumed. To the extent that dead space leads to fewer people on the street (see Haywood 2008; Mehta 2009), its influence may be felt through this highly significant mediating variable. In the urban design qualities survey, the number of people on the street proved the most important determinant of both imageability and complexity (Ewing and Handy 2009). Also important was the presence of outdoor dining, the ultimate in active street frontage. These findings comport with those of Wood, Frank, and Giles-Corti (2010), who observed positive associations between the degree to which buildings front the street (instead of being set back behind parking lots) and residents' sense of community.

Parking lots are the principal source of dead space in urban areas. Many TOD manuals call for reducing off-street parking requirements in areas fully served by transit, and several take particular aim at parking lots. No less authority than William H. Whyte (1988, p. 314) considered parking lots worse than blank walls. Parking lots crowd out active uses, leaving people with fewer reasons to come to an area and park in the first place (Campo and Ryan 2008). Empty metal shells and expanses of flat black asphalt are less interesting than almost any building imaginable (Tunnard and Pushkarev 1963, p. 327).

Building projecting a human presence (Madison, Wisconsin). | *Dan Burden*

Dead spaces of various types (Albuquerque, New Mexico; Spencer, Iowa; Miami, Florida). | *Dan Burden (left and above); Reid Ewing (right)*

Two complementary strategies exist with respect to parking: reduce the amount of it and hide it from view. Experts estimate that 9 percent is the upper limit on the amount of land area that should be devoted to parking; beyond that, people sense that the environment is no longer theirs but instead belongs to automobiles (Alexander, Ishikawa, and Silverstein 1977, pp. 120–25). Downtown pedestrian counts in small cities fall as the amount of open parking increases (Kenyon 1987, pp. 233–37). None of the "great streets" featured in the book by that name has an abundance of parking, either off street or on (A. Jacobs 1993).

Meeting the 9 percent target, or anything like it, is difficult nowadays. At one time, apartments had to have one to one and a half parking spaces per residential unit; now two spaces per unit, or one space for each bedroom, is typical (Center for Neighborhood Technology 2011; Cervero, Adkins, and Sullivan 2009). Similar trends have befallen commercial parking ratios. In suburban jurisdictions, parking is often oversupplied by 30 percent or more relative to peak demands (Ream and Martin 2007; Willson 1995).

To meet the 9 percent target, it is necessary to

- set low minimums and maximums on the amount of parking supplied by developers;
- reduce the amount of parking required whenever land uses with different peaking patterns can share parking areas; for example, retailers with daytime traffic can share parking with movie theaters that are busiest at night (M. Smith 2005);
- give credit for curbside parking against the amount of off-street parking required; and
- substitute parking garages for surface parking lots.

Parking that does not detract from the streetscape (Los Angeles, California). | *Dan Burden*

In *The High Cost of Free Parking*, Donald Shoup (2005) argues for reducing the demand for parking rather than increasing the supply. Among the policies he endorses are initiatives for employers to distribute discounted transit passes, to "cash out" free parking, and to promote car sharing; for residential property owners to unbundle parking from housing costs; and for localities to eliminate minimum parking requirements from zoning ordinances.

Where surface parking remains, it should be placed behind buildings (the best) or to the side (the second best) (Stubbs 2002; Sucher 2003). If placed in front, surface parking should be limited to a row or two to preserve the street orientation of buildings. Peter Calthorpe (1993, p.

110) recommends that parking lots occupy no more than one-third of the frontage on pedestrian-oriented streets, and no more than 75 feet in a single stretch. Even these values may be too high for pedestrian-oriented streets.

Although surface parking lots have the potential to be almost park- or plaza-like, it so seldom happens, in practice. Therefore, screening parking with walls, hedges, or berms is advisable along public streets. Walls can sometimes fit well into urban settings. If low and articulated, they form a nice street edge that is both complex and transparent. In some circumstances, active uses can provide a screen, like Portland, Oregon's use of food stalls, which completely encircle some the city's larger parking lots (Rodgers and Roy 2010).

LOCAL CODE EXAMPLES
Dead Space

Seattle and Fort Worth address two different aspects of preventing dead space in the following code sections. Seattle's code limits parking that is visible from the main street, creating a set of standards and requirements that differ according to the typology of the street. On class I pedestrian streets, parking is only allowed in the rear of buildings or where it is concealed by other uses. On class II pedestrian streets, parking is permitted at street level, but it must be screened from view and 30 percent of it must be separated from the street by other uses, the facade of which must not present as an imposing blank wall. The code from Fort Worth focuses on preventing blank stretches of wall. For new buildings, Fort Worth requires that 25 percent or more of the portion fronting on public streets or spaces have transparent windows.

SEATTLE, WASHINGTON
Land Use Code

A. On Class I pedestrian streets and designated green streets, parking is not permitted at street level unless separated from the street by other uses, provided that garage doors need not be separated.

B. On Class II pedestrian streets, parking may be permitted at street level if:

(1) at least thirty (30) percent of the street frontage of any street level parking area, excluding that portion of the frontage occupied by garage doors, is separated from the street by other uses;

(2) the facade of the separating uses satisfies the transparency and blank wall standards for Class I pedestrian streets for the zone in which the structure is located;

(3) the portion of the parking, excluding garage doors, that is not separated from the street by other uses is screened from view at street level; and

(4) the street facade is enhanced by architectural detailing, artwork, landscaping, or similar visual interest features.

Seattle, Wash., Mun. Code § 23.49.019(B)(1) (2009).

FORT WORTH, TEXAS
Near South Side Development Standards

FENESTRATION (ALL BUILDINGS)—New building facades fronting on publicly accessible streets or other public spaces (except alleys) shall have openings and transparent (not mirrored) glazing that together constitute not less than 25 percent of the facade.

Fort Worth, Tex., Near Southside Dev. Standards and Guidelines § 5.F(5)(c) (2008) (adopted as part of the city code by Fort Worth, Tex., Code appendix A § 4.909(D) (2009)).

High blank wall index (Sarasota, Florida). | *Reid Ewing*

The other major source of dead space in cities is blank walls—windowless or reflective-glass building facades, garage-dominated residential streets, and flat security walls. Although blank walls can define and enclose space, the resulting space is characterless. It takes a combination of doors and windows, architectural details, surface textures, modulation of light and shade, and changes in color to inject life into space and hold pedestrian interest (Gehl, Kaefer, and Reigstad 2006, p. 38).

Whyte (1988, p. 222) considers the idea of calculating a "blank wall index" for urban places, based on the percentage of blank walls up to 30 feet above street level. If such an index were devised and measured over space and time, it would be high in cities, even higher in suburbs, and on the rise everywhere. Based on New York City's experience, it seems reasonable to expect downtowns to have at least 50 percent of their ground-floor frontage devoted to retail uses, and all glass fronts to be of the see-through variety (Whyte 1988, p. 227). Where blank walls are unavoidable, they should be articulated or softened with plantings.

Parking garages, desirable in other respects, add to the blank wall problem of cities. They should be designed to look like neighboring buildings, with the same proportions of vertical and horizontal elements and faced with the same building materials. They should be appropriately landscaped so their appearance becomes less stark. For added interest, parking garages can have retail outlets at street level or retail display cases in their stead. Another option for disguising the blank surfaces of a parking structure is to *wrap* another building around it (Schmitz 2006). Bernard Zyscovich, a Miami-based architect, constructs narrow townhomes and retail along parking garage surfaces and plants gardens in front in order to blend the necessary parking with the more activity-generating development.

The most pedestrian-friendly place in Kansas City, Missouri, is Country Club Plaza. Its parking structures meet these criteria: "The Plaza actually has an abundance of off-street parking to complement the on-street parking, but it is hidden in midblock garages, in garages disguised as buildings, and in garages with street-level retail" (Bohl 2002, p. 45).

LEFT: **Parking structure with street-level retail (Walnut Creek, California); ABOVE: Parking structure designed to look like townhouses (Winter Park, Florida).** | *Dan Burden*

Nearby Parks and Other Public Spaces

LIKE SHOPS, NEARBY PARKS AND OTHER PUBLIC SPACES, such as playgrounds, plazas, gardens, and squares, serve as attractions for pedestrians. People are more likely to walk when they have some place specific, and nearby, to go. Walking around the block, or the subdivision, is a poor substitute for a real destination. Accessibility to public spaces has been linked to physical activity in the public health literature (see meta-analysis by Duncan, Spence, and Mummery 2005; see also Roman and Chalfin 2008; Wolch et al. 2011).

Like city sidewalks, parks and other public spaces serve as settings for casual social interaction and cohesion (Gaffkin, McEldowney, and Sterrett 2010; Peters, Elands, and Buijs 2010). The lack of a sense of community in suburban America is in part due to the lack of settings for neighborly interaction. In his classic *Life between Buildings*, Jan Gehl (1987) posits that when the quality of the built environment is good, optional activities occur with increasing frequency, which in turn increases the number of casual social interactions that likely will occur.

The value of urban parks and public open space has been measured through hedonic price studies, which estimate the added value buyers in real estate markets place on these amenities (Bartholomew and Ewing 2011). Studies have shown that very visible and easily accessible parks are the most valuable to the surrounding community. Consistent with economic theories of scarcity, the studies also show that the value of parks and open space increases with proximity to the city center (Acharya and Bennett 2001; Anderson and West 2006) and that the price effects are stronger for multifamily housing than for detached single-family houses, suggesting that residents of multifamily units place a higher value on park proximity because of their lack of private outdoor spaces (Dehring and Dunse 2006).

Given these positive functions of nearby public open spaces, they might be expected to rank within the first tier of pedestrian- and transit-oriented features, along with wide sidewalks and nearby shops (mixed uses). They are instead placed in the second tier because

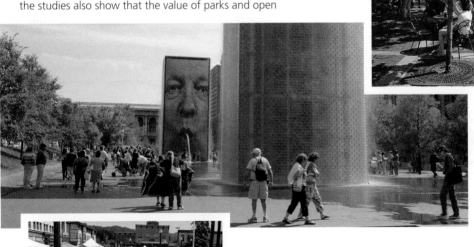

A variety of active public spaces (from lower left: Arcadia, California; Chicago, Illinois; Davis, California).
| *Dan Burden (lower left and above); Millennium Park Inc. (left)*

Public Space

Cambridge, Massachusetts's code provides an interesting mechanism to increase and preserve public space within a redevelopment district. The code provides a density bonus available only with provision of at least 2.2 acres of public open space, half or more to be contiguous and within a designated neighborhood. Additionally, the total open space within the district may not shrink below 100,000 square feet even if the density bonus is not used. The code spells out a choice of property control approaches to ensure that the space remains public for 75 years or longer.

Montgomery, Alabama's public space requirements are very innovative. Montgomery's code uses the idea of a *pedestrian shed*, the quarter-mile radius defining the area within which the average pedestrian can comfortably walk, to describe public space requirements. Under the code set forth below, within certain districts, 5 percent of each pedestrian shed is reserved for public open space, including one primary, centrally located public space. Montgomery's code also requires playgrounds within 1,000 feet of every residential use. By requiring that public spaces border streets, Montgomery's code increases the appeal and likely volume of use of such spaces, since public spaces that appear as extensions of the sidewalk receive more impulsive use and add visual interest and appeal to the street.

CAMBRIDGE, MASSACHUSETTS
Zoning Ordinance

15.41 Public Open Space Requirement. As an incentive for the maximum allowable density as provided in Subsection 15.32.1 there is a requirement that a minimum amount of one hundred thousand (100,000) square feet within the District be permanently reserved or designated (without reference to location) as publicly beneficial open space accessible at ground level as set forth in Section 15.32.5. No development shall be allowed which would permanently reduce publicly beneficial open space in the District below one hundred thousand (100,000) square feet. A minimum of fifty thousand (50,000) square feet of contiguous publicly beneficial open space shall be located west of Sidney Street. The initial location of the required publicly beneficial open space shall be guaranteed through one or more of the following.:

15.41.1 Dedication to and acceptance by the City of Cambridge or other public entity;

15.41.2 Easements or deed restrictions over such land sufficient or ensure that reservation for public open space purposes for at least seventy-five (75) years or longer to the City or other public entity;

15.41.3 Lease agreements of seventy-five (75) years or longer to the City or other public entity;

15.41.4 Dedication, by covenant or comparable legal instrument, enforceable by the City and binding on the owner for seventy-five (75) years or longer.

Cambridge, Mass., Zoning Ord. § 15.41 (2009) (Mun. Code § 17.04.010).

MONTGOMERY, ALABAMA
Zoning Code

A. Each Pedestrian Shed shall assign at least 5% of its urbanized area to Civic Space. . . .

C. Each Pedestrian Shed shall contain at least one main Civic Space. The main Civic Space shall be within 800 feet of the geographic center of each Pedestrian Shed, unless topographic conditions, existing Thoroughfare alignments, or other circumstances require otherwise.

D. Within 1000 feet of every lot in residential use, a Civic Space designed and equipped as a playground shall be provided.

E. Each Civic Space shall have a minimum of 50% of its perimeter enfronting a Thoroughfare.

Montgomery, Ala., Code app. C, art. VI, § 10.14.2 (2007).

parks perform the same functions as these other design features, but do so less effectively. That is, public spaces do not hold as much attraction as shops and do not promote casual neighborly interaction as well as sidewalks (not to mention the use of sidewalks to get around). In this sense, Jane Jacobs's (1961) quip about people giving more to parks than parks giving to people seems apt: "City parks are not abstractions, or automatic repositories of virtue or uplift, any more than sidewalks are abstractions. They mean nothing divorced from their practical, tangible uses, and hence they mean nothing divorced from the tangible effects on them … of the city districts and uses touching them" (p. 145).

For those doubting the truth of that statement, consider the clear preference of children for play in and around streets, particularly dead ends, courts, and culs-de-sac, over play in nearby playgrounds (Veitch et al. 2006). Or consider the crowding in shops along South Beach in Miami, or Park Avenue in Winter Park, Florida, while parks across the street remain only lightly used most of the time. It is no coincidence that all the public places cited by Ray Oldenburg (1991) in *The Great Good Place*—places that host the regular, informal gatherings of individuals—are commercial establishments.

Two design principles follow from the above comparison of public spaces, sidewalks, and shops. First, spaces contribute more to the street environment when they appear as extensions of street and sidewalk rather than as stand-alones (Crankshaw 2009). If a good pedestrian street is an outdoor room, then a good park, playground, or plaza is another room just off the main room, or an alcove within the main room.

Used in this manner, public spaces punctuate the street network, break up long stretches, and grace streets with beginnings and endings. They give the

street on which they sit a special character. They add imageability, complexity, and legibility to the street environment. For some theorists, proximity and access to public and open spaces are two qualities that distinguish compact development forms from urban sprawl (Ewing 1997; Talen 2010).

William H. Whyte's (1988) landmark study of plazas in New York shows just how important connections to the street and sidewalk can be. Well-connected plazas generate a substantial amount of impulse use. Sunken or elevated plazas do not. "If people do not see a space, they will not use it" (p. 128).

The second design principle is that public spaces contribute more to the street environment when they have a variety of land uses nearby rather than drawing on only one use (Talen 2010; Whyte 1988). A single dominant use generates patrons with similar schedules (parents with small children at midafternoon, office workers at lunchtime). Spaces are depopulated at other hours. A generalized space, without any particular draw of its own, is populated naturally only where "life swirls"

ABOVE: **Plaza as extension of the street environment (Boulder, Colorado);** LEFT: **Rittenhouse Square (Philadelphia, Pennsylvania).** | *City of Boulder, Colorado; Adrienne Schmitz*

nearby owing to the interaction of other land uses (J. Jacobs 1961, p. 98). On the other hand, when a park is integrated with an abundance of different surrounding uses, that park will more likely see use at multiple times during the day by many different types of people, reminiscent of Jane Jacobs's famous description of the "ballet of Rittenhouse Square" (1961, pp. 125–26).

Shoppers and other visitors animate public spaces, and public spaces in turn cause them to linger. Spaces can be as small as a flared corner or a recessed entry to a building equipped with a bench and shade tree (Shaftoe 2008). In fact, some of the most valued and heavily used spaces are the smallest, for example Whyte's (1988) beloved Paley Park in New York City, which encompasses only 4,200 square feet. A hint of crowding may actually enhance their appeal and festive character.

Spaces should be highly accessible to pedestrians, linked to other spaces via sight lines, and crammed with activities and sensuous elements, such as trees, water,

and sculpture. Jane Jacobs (1961) relates park use to four elements in their design that she calls intricacy, centering, sun, and enclosure. Enclosure and intricacy are two of our valued urban design qualities, intricacy being equivalent to complexity (see chapter 2). Centering, that is, the presence of a focal point within the park, is part of imageability. A recent review of qualitative research on urban parks identifies safety, aesthetics, amenities, maintenance, proximity, and perceptions of the social environment as important elements affecting individuals' decisions about park use (McCormack et al. 2010).

An experiment in New York City tells much about the conditions that must exist to animate public spaces (Kayden 2000). Before the mid-1970s, developers were granted density bonuses for any outdoor plaza they might provide. Those as-of-right plazas lacked seating, landscaping, ornamental water features, public art, and other amenities. A space-by-space evaluation showed that the great majority of those spaces were devoid of activity.

Since that time, density bonuses have been contingent on the location, orientation, shape, proportion, ele-

Plaza at Herald Square (New York, New York). | *34th Street Partnership*

vation, and functional and aesthetic amenities of spaces. Seating, landscaping, and night lighting are provided at a high proportion of spaces. Artwork, bicycle facilities, drinking fountains, tables, food services, restrooms, and other amenities are common. The newer plazas do not create undesirable gaps in the enclosing street wall. "Not surprisingly, field surveys of post-1975 outdoor spaces show substantially greater numbers of users compared with previously provided outdoor spaces" (Kayden 2000, p. 54).

The key requirement seems to be seating. Starting in the mid-1970s, New York zoning began requiring one linear foot of seating for every 30 square feet of urban plaza. William H. Whyte (1988) discovered that what most distinguishes the populated plazas from the empty ones is their ample, comfortable seating (p. 112). People seem to prefer seating opportunities located at the edge of large areas of activity, and they will consistently choose to sit in places oriented toward and with views of adjacent areas filled with other people (Gehl 1987, p.159).

Small-Scale Buildings (or Articulated Larger Ones)

WHEN DESIGNERS CALL FOR SMALL- OR HUMAN-SCALE BUILDINGS along public streets, they are referring to scale in two dimensions, vertical and horizontal. Vertically, buildings should not be so tall as to completely block the pedestrian's cone of vision. The street space becomes canyon-like and no direct sunlight reaches the pedestrian zone. Likewise, buildings should not be so horizontally massive along the street as to isolate building occupants from easy access to other land uses and the casual interaction that occurs along the street.

How tall is too tall? One source has set the limit of human scale at three stories, another at four, a third at six (Alexander, Ishikawa, and Silverstein 1977, pp. 114–19; H. Blumenfeld 1967, pp. 217–18; Lennard 2008). At

three or four stories, the intersection of building and sky still registers in the pedestrian's peripheral vision. With a slight tilt of the head, the pedestrian can take in the entire building facade. The occupant of the uppermost

Good building height and density (Boca Raton, Florida). | *Reid Ewing*

LEFT: **Building designed to break up horizontal dimension (Charlotte, North Carolina);** ABOVE: **Not entirely authentic, but walkable and bikeable town center (Miami Lakes, Florida).** | *Dan Burden; Reid Ewing*

floor may still feel part of the street scene—see details on the street, call down to someone, quickly walk down to engage in street activities.

The three- or four-story limit is subject to a caveat. As discussed previously, pedestrians will experience a sense of street enclosure only where buildings are sufficiently tall in relation to street widths. The "great streets" studied by Allan Jacobs (1993, p. 281) include some wide avenues and boulevards that are sometimes bounded by tall buildings with many more stories, some as tall as 100 feet. Given the width of the streets, this scale of buildings is appropriate. A careful balance must always be maintained between human scale and the scale of the setting.

As for the horizontal dimension of buildings, no simple rule of thumb, like the four-story rule, is available to define small scale. But in traditional urban settings, one thinks of buildings as having dominant vertical proportions (Jacobs and Appleyard 1987). In other words, buildings wider than they are tall will seem incongruent and out of place, indicating that building widths of 30 to 100 feet, depending on their heights, are desirable.

The horizontal dimension of buildings may actually be more important than the vertical. Narrow buildings keep eyes engaged by introducing the work of multiple architects and exposing many building surfaces. Wide buildings that extend the length of the street provide little of visual interest to pedestrians unless the ground floor is broken up into narrower, subdivided uses. These elements help define street space and subdivide long

streets by providing many vertical lines against which scale can be judged.

The horizontal dimension may also make the street edge more transparent by increasing the number of entrances facing the street, and usually the number of windows as well. The modern office building typically features a single grand entrance into the lobby area, leaving the remaining building facade as dead space along the street. For these reasons, the presence of many narrow buildings along the street is considered, by two leading authorities, to be among the five most important qualities of good urban design (Jacobs and Appleyard 1987). An urban fabric replete with narrow buildings and numerous entrances tends to support an economically and culturally resilient *civic ecosystem* (Childs 2001, 2009) and the fine-grained mixed-use environment outlined in chapter 3. It also provides greater opportunity for the interspersing of mixed-age buildings, which Jane Jacobs (1961, p. 187) lists as one

Human scale with taller building stepping back from the street (Clarendon, Virginia). | *Reid Ewing*

Building Scale and Mass

These two codes, from Salt Lake City, Utah, and San Antonio, Texas, focus on incorporating smaller, human-scale characteristics into large buildings. Salt Lake City's code does not restrict overall building size but requires that building facades in developments exceeding 60,000 square feet have articulated exteriors, and it suggests approaches such as patterns and sheltering roofs. The code also limits the amount of uninterrupted building width, although the limitation only applies to buildings in excess of the already-lengthy 300 feet. San Antonio's code explicitly emphasizes the need for human scale, calling for a pattern of windows, doors, and architectural features that are cohesive and aligned with adjacent facades. The code requires that commercial and mixed-use facilities visually distinguish between upper and lower floors, and that ground floors contain a high percentage of windows. The code also requires that, for buildings exceeding given lengths (between 30 and 100 feet, depending on location), street- and riverside facades be divided into traditionally scaled modules.

SALT LAKE CITY, UTAH

Zoning Code

The following additional standards shall apply to any large scale developments with a gross floor area exceeding sixty thousand (60,000) square feet:

1. The orientation and scale of the development shall conform to the following requirements:

A. Large building masses shall be divided into heights and sizes that relate to human scale by incorporating changes in building mass or direction, sheltering roofs, a distinct pattern of divisions on surfaces, windows, trees, and small scale lighting.

B. No new buildings or contiguous groups of buildings shall exceed a combined contiguous building length of three hundred feet (300').

Salt Lake City, Utah, Code § 21A.59.060(M) (2009).

SAN ANTONIO, TEXAS

Unified Development Code

Mass and Scale. A building should appear to have a "human scale." In general, this scale can be accomplished by using familiar forms and elements interpreted in human dimensions. Exterior wall designs should help pedestrians establish a sense of scale with relation to each building. Articulating the number of floors in a building can help to establish a building's scale, for example, and prevent larger buildings from dwarfing the pedestrian.

(1) Express facade components in ways that will help to establish building scale.

A. Treatment of architectural facades should contain a discernible pattern of mass to void, or windows and doors to solid mass. Openings should appear in a regular pattern, or be clustered to form a cohesive design. Architectural elements such as columns, lintels, sills, canopies, windows and doors should align with other architectural features on the adjacent facades.

(2) Align horizontal building elements with others in the blockface to establish building scale.

A. Align at least one (1) horizontal building element with another horizontal building element on the same block face. It will be considered to be within alignment if it is within three (3) feet, measured vertically, of the existing architectural element.

(3) Express the distinction between upper and lower floors in commercial and mixed-use buildings.

A. Develop the first floor as primarily transparent. The building facade facing a major street shall have at least thirty (30) percent of the street level facade area devoted to display windows and/or windows affording some view into the interior areas. Multi-family residential buildings with no retail or office space are exempt from this requirement.

(4) Where a building facade faces the street or river and exceeds the maximum facade length allowed in Table 674-1 [30 to 100 feet] divide the facade of building into modules that express traditional dimensions.

San Antonio, Tex., Unified Dev. Code art. VI, div. 6, §§ 35-674(b)(1)–(4) (2009).

---

of the elements required for a socially vibrant street environment.

Although human-scale buildings are the ideal, large buildings can be made to appear less massive if divided into many smaller forms through articulated architecture (Macdonald 2005). Richard Hedman (1984) devotes much

of his *Fundamentals of Urban Design* to coping with oversized city buildings (pp. 20–21, 44–51, 60–70, 105-35). Changes in exterior building materials can be used to disguise the true width of buildings; cornices and belt courses can mitigate the height. Awnings, balconies, and other projections can reduce the perceived mass of buildings.

Main Street in Miami Lakes, Florida, is lined with a few long buildings, with shops at the street level and apartments above. The buildings feel like many small, attached structures due to their projections, angled surfaces, varying roof lines, and facades painted in different, but complementary colors. Miami Lakes Town Center and other unified development projects like it have been criticized for lacking the organic character and social class diversity of real downtowns. But for pure walkability, this place easily beats many real downtowns.

Where buildings are much taller than ideal for pedestrians, they can be designed as two or more separate building types within the same envelope. For Roger Trancik (1986), "the only way the integrity of street can be preserved in a city of towers is by making clear transitions from high to low building elements" (p. 39). The base can spread out, giving human-scale definition to streets and plazas, while upper floors step back before they ascend.

Pedestrian-Scale Lighting

LIGHTING FOR PEDESTRIANS IS MOST EFFECTIVELY PROVIDED BY PEDESTRIAN-SCALE STREETLIGHTS. Pedestrian-scale lighting is lower in height (12–16 feet) than standard streetlighting and is spaced closer together (about 60 feet) than standard streetlighting. Fixtures often have better aesthetics than freeway-style cobra-head lights. Along streets under 45 feet wide, pedestrian-scale lighting can also provide adequate roadway lighting. Wider streets may require additional illumination to meet IESNA (Illuminating Engineering Society of North America) standards (www.iesna.org).

As an item of street furniture placed just inside the curb, ornamental pedestrian streetlights may contribute to several valued urban design qualities: imageability, human scale, enclosure, complexity, and coherence of streetscapes. Although lighting may not perform those functions as well as street trees, a combination of closely spaced trees and pedestrian-scale streetlights works particularly well. Charlotte, North Carolina's *Urban Street Design Guidelines* suggests filling the "pedestrian area" with a combination of street trees and pedestrian-oriented streetlights (Charlotte Department of Transportation 2007, p. 32).

Lighting that focuses on the sidewalk and shines down rather than out allows people to make out details of others walking toward them, increasing the feeling of security and encouraging people to use an

Pedestrian-scale lighting that also lights the street (Charlottesville, Virginia; Shanghai, China)
| *Jack Looney Photography; Shui On Land*

area at night. Lower and more closely spaced fixtures distribute light evenly along a sidewalk, avoiding alternating bright and shadowed areas that lead to perceptions of danger. In addition to eliminating dark areas, pedestrian-scale lighting offers better visibility with a reduced overall level of light, since a person's ability to adapt to darkness is improved. Streetlights at transit stations and bus stops should illuminate the area evenly, avoiding excessive brightness or deep shadows (Lohan Associates 1996).

Pedestrians are the most vulnerable population on the roads at night, and adequate streetlighting can significantly improve their safety and security (Rea et al. 2009). Approximately two-thirds of pedestrian collision fatalities occur at night or under low-light conditions (Zegeer et al. 2010). The absence of streetlights increases the probability of pedestrian fatality by as much as 400 percent (Kim et al. 2010). Elvik (1995) and Wanvik (2009) estimate that streetlighting can reduce pedestrian crashes at night by 50 percent or more.

In a number of evaluations of streetlighting improvements, crime and fear of crime were assessed using attitudinal and behavioral measures, through before-and-after surveys of pedestrians. Streetlighting was upgraded along urban streets and pedestrian footpaths. The studies provide convincing evidence that sensitively deployed streetlighting can lead to reductions in crime and fear of crime, and increases in pedestrian street use

Tree canopy above pedestrian-scale lights (Takoma Park, Maryland). | *Dan Burden*

after dark (Farrington and Welsh 2002; Jago et al. 2005; Merom et al. 2009; Reynolds et al. 2007).

The IESNA suggests average light levels of two foot-candles for sidewalks in "high pedestrian conflict areas" (DiLaura 2011). These levels are substantially higher than those recommended for roadways themselves. Even higher light levels, 3.4 foot-candles, are recommended for major intersections and midblock crosswalks. Sight triangles at intersections and other crossing locations should be fully illuminated per AASHTO (2005) guidelines. Lighting is critical at pedestrian crossing islands,

LOCAL CODE EXAMPLES: Streetlighting

Nashville, Tennessee's code requires that lighting be designed and located at a pedestrian scale. It specifies that lighting should be shielded to avoid glare and acknowledges the aesthetic function of lighting by requiring compatibility with surrounding properties. Rather than stating that lighting should be pedestrian scale, language that is subject to varying interpretations, San Antonio, Texas's code specifies that pedestrian-oriented lighting is not to exceed 15 feet in height.

NASHVILLE, TENNESSEE
Zoning Code

Lighting shall be designed and located at a pedestrian scale consistent with pedestrian movements and the neighborhood. Lighting shall be concealed or shielded to avoid glare and off-site impacts on abutting properties. Lighting poles and fixtures shall be compatible with the function and design of the feature and abutting properties.

Nashville and Davidson County Tenn., Code part II, tit. 17, ch. 17.36, art. IV, § 17.40.160(F)(3) (2009).

SAN ANTONIO, TEXAS
Unified Development Code

Provide Lighting for Pedestrian Ways That is Low Scaled for Walking.

A. The position of a lamp in a pedestrian-way light should not exceed fifteen (15) feet in height above the ground.

San Antonio, Tex., Unified Dev. Code art. VI, div. 6, § 35-673(j)(2) (2009).

including their approach ends, so that both drivers and pedestrians can grasp the general layout.

The color of light coming from a fixture is important for creating a more welcoming nighttime environment. The Federal Highway Administration recommends pedestrian lighting with white light as opposed to yellowish sodium lamps used in freeway-style cobra-head lights. White light can be achieved with mercury-vapor, metal-halide, or incandescent fixtures; low-pressure sodium lights are undesirable because they create distortion.

Streetlights are frequently obscured by tree canopies. Many species do not grow tall enough to allow them to be trimmed very high above the sidewalk. Tree types with higher canopies or less dense foliage along with lower fixture heights will enable sidewalks to be fully illuminated when the trees are in full leaf (see "Closely Spaced Shade Trees" in this chapter).

Conventionally, most lighting recommendations consider only safety and visibility. Possible effects from light pollution also need to be considered, however. The International Dark-Sky Association and Illuminating Engineering Society have developed a model lighting ordinance that provides guidance on pedestrian-scale lighting standards that conserve energy; minimize adverse effects, including glare, light trespass, and sky glow. Goals include preserving the dark night sky for astronomy and helping protect the natural environment from the adverse effects of night lighting from electric sources (IDA and IESNA 2011).

Attractive Transit Facilities

IN THE QUEST FOR EFFICIENCY, transit has become dull and utilitarian, part of the problem rather than the solution to today's lifeless streetscapes (Cappe 1991). Benches are covered with advertising. Plexiglass shelters project a cheap, second-class image. Some transfer centers and park-and-ride lots are stark to the point of unsightliness. With their dark tinted windows and unbroken horizontal lines, standard transit coaches are mobile versions of the dark, reflective-glass buildings that urban designers rail against.

Results of our visual preference survey provide insights into what people consider *classy* and *classless* in transit facilities (Ewing 2000). In the paired comparison of bus stops, scenes were more likely to be chosen when advertising was absent from benches and shelters. This choice was true for transit users, nonusers, and transit professionals. In addition to aesthetic reasons, these responses may also be tied to security concerns, given the degree to which advertising sometimes interferes with bus shelter visibility and surveillance (Texas Transportation Institute 1996).

In the separate slide show of bus shelters, higher ratings were given to shelters with some architectural flair, whether by virtue of spacious designs, pitched roofs, or traditional materials, such as brick and metal. Interestingly, opinions diverged between transit professionals and non-transit-users, on the one hand, and transit users on the other. Transit professionals and nonusers seemed to care more about shelter appearance, whereas transit users were more concerned about weather protection. This factor is one reason why "Comfortable and Safe Places to Wait" (see chapter 3) ranks in the first tier of pedestrian- and transit-oriented features, whereas "Attractive Transit Facilities" is assigned to the second tier.

Rather than being viewed as transportation infrastructure alone, transit benches, shelters, and even buses should be viewed as items of street furniture (Texas Transportation Institute 1996). Yes, even buses are street furniture, albeit a mobile version. They can and should be designed to enhance streetscapes. In some cases, transit operators might do better by putting fewer buses on the street at times of low demand and diverting the money they save into bus stop amenities and fleet facelifts.

Many transit operators are using minibuses or rubber-tired trolleys. Boulder, Colorado, has used buses that are both visually striking and user-friendly. The transit network also creatively named the bus routes Hop, Skip, Jump, Leap, Bound, Dash, and Stampede (Dunphy et al. 2004).

Given the quantitative nature of most shelter design standards, the significant variation in the design of shelters actually produced is remarkable. The variations include a rather robust array of unusual and amusing shelter types, demonstrating a relative degree of flexibil-

LOCAL CODE EXAMPLES

Transit Facilities

Minneapolis's code uses an incentive system to provide a much more comprehensive set of requirements for the functionality and usability of the transit stop itself. Developers can obtain FAR premiums by building and maintaining transit facilities that meet a number of requirements. Facilities must include heat, light, and shelter, and must provide high visibility. In addition, facilities must contain resting spaces for 30 percent of the projected peak demand and must be visually tied into related principal structures. These requirements reflect weather and comfort features necessary to accommodate transit riders year-round in Minneapolis. San Diego's code requires that transit stops be attractive and visible and provide shelter from the elements. The code also requires that developments along transit corridors include bicycle parking, benches, and other user-friendly features.

MINNEAPOLIS, MINNESOTA
Zoning Code

Transit facility, subject to the following standards:

A. The transit facility shall be located at a transit stop location approved by the planning director in consultation with the city engineer. The maximum transit facility premium shall be increased by one (1) where the transit facility is located at an approved light rail transit stop.

B. The transit facility shall be open to the general public at least during the normal hours of transit service.

C. The transit facility shall be similar to the principal structure in design and materials, shall be weather protected, heated and lighted, and shall contain at least two (2) entries.

D. The transit facility shall be clearly visible from the street and sidewalk, and transit users shall be able to see oncoming transit vehicles from the facility.

E. The transit facility shall contain a combination of leaning rails and seating for at least thirty (30) percent of projected peak demand, trash receptacles and connections for transit schedule monitors.

F. The transit facility shall be maintained in good order for the life of the principal structure.

Minneapolis, Minn., Code tit. 20, ch. 549, § 549.220(5) (2009).

SAN DIEGO, CALIFORNIA | PLANNED DISTRICTS CHAPTER
Municipal Code

(2) Design transit stops to be attractive, highly visible and provide shelter. Transit stop design and location should be acceptable to MTDB [Metropolitan Transit Development Board].

(3) Include transit shelters, bicycle parking facilities, canopies, patterned sidewalks, information kiosks, benches and other pedestrian amenities in developments located along transit corridors. Enhanced transit shelters are desirable.

San Diego, Cal., Mun. Code §§ 1514.0408(j)(2)–(3) (2009).

ity in how shelter standards are interpreted, which has spurred a number of shelter design competitions, like those sponsored in Oklahoma City (AIA 2006) and Salt Lake City (Warburton 2006).

The Federal Transit Administration's publication *Art in Transit ... Making It Happen* encourages transit agencies to incorporate public art into their systems and many transit agencies in the United States have done so (FTA 1996). Public art may be integrated into functional components, such as shelters, benches, leaning rails, and light poles. According to one source, "Public art, in particular, has played an increasingly recognized role in its ability to link facilities to communities while giving new life to ordinary transit structures and vehicles" (Project for Public Spaces/Multisystems 1999, p. 8).

Park City, Utah, has custom-designed bus shelters that reflect the character of nearby trip generators, such as a school-themed one near a school. Additionally, an international online *crowdsourcing* competition has been used to select efficient and artistic transit shelter designs for Salt Lake City (McKone 2010). Seattle, Washington's Metro created the Metro Bus Shelter Mural Program

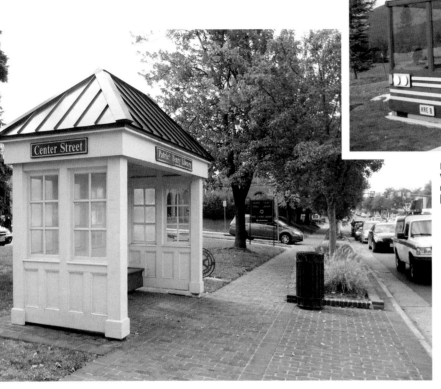

LEFT: **Bus shelter with style (Fairfax County, Virginia);** ABOVE: **Whimsical bus shelter near a school (Park City, Utah).**
| *Adrienne Schmitz; Reid Ewing*

to upgrade its bus shelters. The program uses etched art glass to discourage graffiti on the shelter's glass and involves youth and other residents in painting and designing shelters. Since the start of the program in the late 1980s, over 700 murals have been created in bus shelters.

On a much larger scale, the Transbay Joint Powers Authority in San Francisco is working to integrate art into the architectural design of the new Transbay Transit Center, commissioning major works by artists James Carpenter, Julie Chang, Jenny Holzer, and Ned Kahn. The intent of the center's art program is to "shape the character of a new mixed-use neighborhood around the Transit Center through meaningful references to San Francisco's history, culture, architectural heritage, and natural environment" (Ayerdi-Kaplan and Clarke 2011, p. 1). This systems-level initiative parallels earlier work done in the design and construction of the MetroLink system in St. Louis, where a team of artists collaborated with engineers and architects in the design of the entire rail system (E. Blumenfeld and Yatzeck 1996).

Overall, the objective of all these initiatives is to incorporate into the design of transit vehicles and facilities elements that contribute positively to the user's experience of place, to mitigate negative aesthetic elements, and to promote community development.

The features outlined in this chapter, although not as central as those covered in the previous chapter, are nevertheless important to the creation of good pedestrian environments. As emphasized throughout this book, making places comfortable and functional for pedestrians is an incremental, cumulative endeavor, requiring the interlacing of numerous synergistic elements. Invariably, the successful places represent outcomes that are greater than the sums of their individual parts.

CHAPTER 5

CHECKLIST
of Worthwhile Additions

- Landmarks
- Street walls
- Functional street furniture
- Coherent, small-scale signage
- Special pavement
- Public art
- Water features
- Outdoor dining
- Underground utilities

This chapter presents the third checklist of urban design features. Though not as important as those described in chapters 3 and 4, these features still play a meaningful role in creating a suitable environment for pedestrians and transit users.

Landmarks

THE GOLDEN GATE BRIDGE AND THE EIFFEL TOWER are iconic landmarks that nearly define the term, but landmarks can be anything from unique signage to a distant skyscraper. In the simplest terms, landmarks are points of reference for wayfinding. They can be any built or natural object that is easy to recognize, like a monument, building, or other structure that has notable physical features or historical significance. Landmarks typically contrast with the surrounding buildings and landscapes, whether by texture, size, color, age, or spatial prominence. In the pedestrian environment, their unique qualities create identity and character.

Kevin Lynch's *The Image of the City* (1960) serves as a reference point for the discussion of landmarks. Landmarks, according to Lynch, can give reassurance to wayfinders by creating familiarity, as well as provide a symbolic image that can define a region or town. He cautions that landmarks can "dwarf or throw out of scale a small region at its base," and when standing in contrast to the character of an area, they can either intensify or destroy the continuity (p. 84). Landmarks need to be part of a whole, with paths, edges, and nodes all playing into their importance and significance. Any breaks in transportation routes that serve as decision points for travelers are areas of heightened perception and ideal places for properly designed landmarks. When correctly designed and

LEFT AND BELOW: **Iconic images create local identity (Indianapolis, Indiana; Santa Fe, New Mexico); BOTTOM: A natural landmark (Crested Butte, Colorado).** | *Dan Burden (left and bottom); Adrienne Schmitz (below)*

placed, they are invaluable for recognition and memorization of routes.

The qualities that define a landmark often depend on one's mode of travel. For pedestrians, a landmark could be as simple as a doorknob or as grandiose as the tallest skyscraper. For transit riders, historical buildings or sculptures can serve as landmarks. The transit stations themselves are landmarks and may be enhanced with public art or items of historic significance that help identify them. Landmarks do not need to be constructed: in many cities and towns, mountains or water bodies serve as the primary landmarks. These contrasting built or natural objects serve as reference points for visitors and residents alike. Interestingly, in some cases the landmarks need not be seen to provide a useful wayfinding function: in many cities, people orient in reference to the direction of the ocean, the river, or the lake, even when they cannot see the water directly.

In *The Image of the City*, Lynch uses the gold dome of Boston's State House as an example of a distant landmark. The building is dominant on the general skyline and can be used as a wayfinding or route-selecting tool. The base of distant landmarks is not nearly as important as their top. It is their "floating quality" that helps orient pedestrians from afar. The visibility, recognizability, placement, and symbolic importance of the gold dome make the State House an important landmark for central Boston.

A lesser-known series of landmarks in Radnor, Pennsylvania, creates a powerful wayfinding system for Radnor

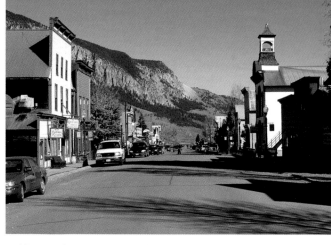

residents. After concern over the construction of a new highway through Radnor, officials sought the help of artists to enhance a five-mile stretch of the new roadway. Stone mile markers were placed along the route, serving as signposts for automobiles. As one draws closer to the center of the town, the objects get larger, culminating with a 120-foot rock formation marking the entrance to the city from the new highway (Fleming 2007).

Textured pavement and eye-level murals are also used as local landmarks. In *The Art of Placemaking*, Ronald Lee Fleming (2007) showcases a bronze map inlay created for the symbolic entrance to Bronzeville, a historic African American neighborhood on Chicago's South

Side. The bronze finish stands in contrast to the surrounding pavement and complements a nearby statue. Viewers can use this wayfinding element to locate historic, cultural, and other significant neighborhood sites.

The importance of landmarks to physical orientation and wayfinding is confirmed by a wide body of cognitive science literature. In one representative study, researchers asked 90 study participants to walk a complex route through an unfamiliar city using maps that had differing numbers of landmarks represented. As the number of landmarks increased from zero to 143, participants' wayfinding success rate increased from 30 to 100 percent, far outstripping the effectiveness rates of other variables (Higashiyama 2008). Other studies in recent years have shown similar results.

Landmarks have been relegated to the third tier of pedestrian-oriented places because prominent buildings, memorable architecture, and public art did not register as significant contributors to imageability in our study of urban design qualities (Ewing and Handy 2009). Instead, Lynch's quality of imageability was a function of less spectacular features, such as the number of people on the street; the number of courtyards, plazas, and parks; the presence of outdoor dining; and the number of major landscape features. The lack of significance of landmarks forces us to rethink just what makes a place memorable.

ABOVE: **Denver's riverfront provides a reference point for the downtown;** LEFT: **Pedestrian-scale landmark (Charleston, South Carolina).** | *East West Partners; Dan Burden*

Landmarks

Washington, D.C.'s code spells out the value of landmarks and calls for their protection and enhancement. In contrast, Aurora, Colorado's code calls for public spaces that are memorable and accessible and that offer a place where people can gather. The code will likely lead to sites that people identify with a place and may create lovely meeting points and reference points for travel orientation, although those places may not rise to the order of historic or monumental landmarks.

WASHINGTON, D.C.

District of Columbia District Code

It is hereby declared as a matter of public policy that the protection, enhancement, and perpetuation of properties of historical, cultural, and esthetic merit are in the interests of the health, prosperity, and welfare of the people of the District of Columbia. Therefore, this subchapter is intended to:

(1) Effect and accomplish the protection, enhancement, and perpetuation of improvements and landscape features of landmark districts which represent distinctive elements of the city's cultural, social, economic, political, and architectural history;

(2) Safeguard the city's historic, aesthetic and cultural heritage, as embodied and reflected in such landmarks to next search terms and districts;

(3) Foster civic pride in the accomplishments of the past;

(4) Protect and enhance the city's attraction to visitors and the support and stimulus to the economy thereby provided; and

(5) Promote the use of landmarks and historic districts for the education, pleasure, and welfare of the people of the District of Columbia.

D.C. Code § 6-1101(a) (2009).

AURORA, COLORADO

Building and Zoning Code

Plazas, main streets, squares or open space are used to create enduring and memorable public spaces. These spaces are part of a highly integrated system of streets, walkways, and buildings that create a sense of enclosure on the street where citizens walk, recreate, congregate and interact. These spaces use interesting entryways and features. Intense uses around these spaces will activate them and make them lively. The public spaces are adjacent or well-connected to the transit station. Outdoor commercial activities, such as outdoor restaurant seating, will be encouraged as part of the transition between wholly public outdoor space and wholly private building space.

Aurora, Colo., Building and Zoning Code ch. 146, art. 7, div. 6, § 146-728(F)(1) (2009).

Street Walls

DESIGNERS SPEAK OF *STREET WALLS* IN ALMOST REVERENTIAL TERMS (for example, see Duany and Plater-Zyberk 1992). A street wall consists of uninterrupted building facades with only slightly varying setbacks and heights. Examples include the storefronts along the main street of small-town America and the rowhouses of the traditional city.

The most important feature of street walls is visual enclosure, a pedestrian-oriented quality that is discussed at some length in chapter 2. If uninterrupted facades exist on both sides of a street, if buildings are of comparable height, and if the street is not too wide, observers will perceive the facades as the sidewalls of an outdoor room, and the sky as an invisible ceiling resting on them (Forsyth, Jacobson, and Thering 2010). In our urban de-

sign qualities study (Ewing and Handy 2009), the proportion of street frontage in the form of a street wall was significant as a determinant of both enclosure and transparency. Street walls are, naturally, created in part by having street-oriented buildings, as described in chapter 3. Consistently building up to the sidewalk property line is the primary method for creating street walls (Sucher 2003, p. 47), which is why most form-based codes have

Street walls in commercial and residential districts (Cedar Falls, Iowa; Lake Nona, Florida). | *Dan Burden; Lake Nona Property Holdings LLC*

build-to lines as a central feature, rather than setbacks as mandated in many older codes.

Street walls would be higher up on the list of pedestrian- and transit-oriented features were it not for two facts. First, street walls, by themselves, have no special ability to enliven or populate street space. The downtown financial centers of many U.S. cities have excellent street walls, but they lack vitality, in large part because they lack active uses at the ground floor (Robertson 1993). Indeed, unrelentingly uniform street walls, when extended too high, can feel claustrophobic and cut pedestrians off from air and light, which is why even the earliest zoning ordinances (for example, New York

Street Walls

On designated pedestrian-oriented streets, Seattle's code requires that each building's facade be built to the street property line for 70 percent of the building's length. Peoria, Illinois's code is similar but provides more detailed specifications. Peoria's code has the more demanding requirement that 80 percent of the facade be built to the required building line, but it provides flexibility by allowing jogs of 18 inches to accommodate architectural details, such as bay windows, shopfronts, and the like. The required building line is frequently the same as the street property line, but it need not be. Peoria also ensures that the street wall prevails at street corners by requiring that the facade be built out to the required building line within 30 feet of a corner.

SEATTLE, WASHINGTON
Land Use Code

All facades on Class 1 Pedestrian Streets, as shown on Map B, shall be built to the street property line along a minimum of seventy (70) percent of the facade length (Exhibit 23.48.014 A [PICTURE].

Seattle, Wash., Mun. Code tit. 23, subtit. 3, div. 2, ch. 23.48, § 23.48.014 (C) (2009).

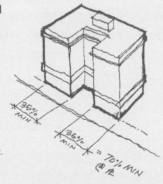

PEORIA, ILLINOIS | LAND DEVELOPMENT CODE
Street Facade

A. On each lot the building facade shall be built to the required building line for at least 80% of the required building line length.
B. The building facade shall be built to the required building line (RBL) within 30 feet of a block corner.
C. These portions of the building facade (the required minimum build-to) may include jogs of not more than 18 inches in depth except as otherwise provided to allow bay windows, shopfronts, and balconies.
Peoria, Ill., Code app. C, § 6.2(A)(9) (2009).

Fill Corners with Attractive, Lively Uses

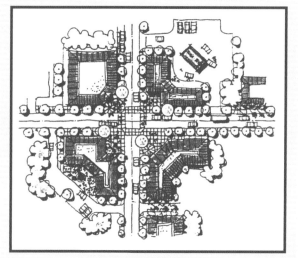

Source: Glatting Jackson Kercher Anglin Lopez Rinehart Inc. 1994; p. 7.4.

RIGHT: **Staggered setbacks for variety and identity (Issaquah Highlands, Washington); BELOW: Traditional neighborhood of detached homes (Daybreak, Utah).** | *©Fusionhappen; Reid Ewing*

City's Zoning Resolution of 1916) mandated street wall setbacks that increase as building height increases (Kiefer 2001). Second, many vibrant urban places have buildings arranged in ways other than traditional street walls. Regularly spaced detached buildings can have appealing street orientation (Crankshaw 2009). Some staggering of setbacks may add to visual interest, as is the case in much of the Back Bay neighborhood in Boston, and along Riverside Drive in New York City (Bressi 1995). Any traditional neighborhood of porch-fronted homes fails the street wall test but certainly qualifies as pedestrian oriented.

Having opened the door to other building arrangements, screening out those arrangements that will

not work is necessary. Buildings cannot stand too far apart without losing continuity of the streetscape (Abramson 2008; Garvin 2000; Laurence 2006; Price 2000). Buildings should edge up to street corners so the corners, at least, become positive spaces. Exposed sides of detached buildings should be as transparent and architecturally interesting as the fronts. Trees should be used liberally along streets with discontinuous buildings to help create a virtual street wall. Driveways should be kept to an absolute minimum. Pedestrians should not need to dodge, nor worry about dodging, cars turning into or out of individual driveways.

Functional Street Furniture

IT IS HARD TO DRAW A BEAD ON THE SIGNIFICANCE OF STREET FURNITURE. Supporters of streetscape programs assert that without seating, lighting, planters, and so on, streets act only as routes rather than cultivating the diversity of activities found in destination public spaces. Critics, on the other hand, view the role of street furniture as largely cosmetic. Elegant benches and colorful banners cannot create a sense of place, says one designer; a sense of place requires a sense of space, well-defined public space (Duany and Plater-Zyberk 1992). Others add that too much emphasis is placed on harmonizing street furniture when most street users will hardly notice it. Even granting its status as dessert rather than the main course, street furniture may deserve more credit than it sometimes receives. In our own visual preference survey, the number of distinct pieces of street furniture visible in a scene proved a significant contributor to perceived human scale (Ewing and Handy 2009). The book *City Comforts* (Sucher 2003) is filled with examples of how street furniture, cleverly designed and displayed, has added to the livability of that most livable city, Seattle. Appropriately scaled and positioned benches and other street furniture can add to the comfort level of pedestrians (Capella 1998); an inordinate number of "great streets" are equipped with benches and other street furniture (A. Jacobs 1993, pp. 299–301). Street furniture can help differentiate streets, giving them an identity (Hartnett 2008). In sum, street furniture can make at least modest contributions to many qualities of good urban design, including imageability, human scale, complexity, coherence, and comfort (chapter 2). It can also assist in providing a buffer between the sidewalk and the street (chapter 3).

In *The Art of Placemaking*, Fleming (2007, p. 244) devotes an entire chapter to street furniture as "an armature for placemaking." "Good street furniture may not 'make' a place," he intones, "but it can certainly add meaning." Fleming advocates artist-designed street furniture that tells specific stories about their sites. Examples of locally designed street furniture, documented by Michael Wolf (2008) in his photo essay "Sitting in China," demonstrate how makeshift chairs on the backstreets of Chinese cities have been improvised and personalized by the people living in surrounding neighborhoods. Although these examples are a far cry from citywide coordination programs, they reveal that street furniture can be functional and artistic while still giving the user freedom to rearrange the space.

Informal street furniture similar to that in Wolf's photo essay has become common practice in many forward-thinking cities as a method for experimenting with temporary public space. Movable tables and chairs provide a quick way to turn such spaces as parking spots, medians, or vacant lots into parks while encouraging pedestrians to realize inventive new uses for familiar spaces. Cities like Birmingham, Alabama, Miami, Florida, and New York City have experimented with cheap, movable furniture, such as plastic foldable and Adirondack chairs that allow users to create and modify their own spaces.

The success of temporary furniture influenced the New York City Department of Transportation to transform the chaotic, traffic-filled streets in Times and Herald Squares into vibrant pedestrian spaces. The area has become a destination for outdoor dining and convening through the city's implementation of creative surface paving and movable furniture and has reframed pedestrian ownership of the space.

Fleming's observations are supported by several studies, including research on *street parks* in Bergen, Norway. Street parks—the Norwegian equivalent of the Dutch *woonerven*—are short sections of residential streets that, through the use of alternative paving surfaces and street furniture, are converted to outdoor living spaces with limited access for driving and parking cars. Using a series of pre- and post-test surveys, as

Street furniture helps create a sense of place (Arlington, Virginia; Amarillo, Texas; Orlando, Florida). | *Adrienne Schmitz; Melissa Dailey; Dan Burden*

LOCAL CODE EXAMPLES

Street Furniture

San Antonio's code features a number of excellent provisions regarding street furniture. The code calls for a variety of different seating options, supports physical activity by encouraging drinking fountains, and calls for inconspicuous but convenient trash cans. Recognizing the important aesthetic and place-making role of street furniture, the code notes that street furniture should not be uniform, but should complement the distinctive nature of the district in which it is located. San Antonio also requires a clear path without obstacles for walking and suggests clustering different types of street furniture to increase use, create friendly gathering spots, and avoid clutter.

San Diego's street furniture code language focuses on benches and their appearance, requiring that benches be wood or iron, rather than plastic, and prohibiting advertisements on benches located in the right-of-way. The code also requires that street furniture not intrude into the wide sidewalk and regulates the positioning of benches to allow socializing and people watching.

SAN ANTONIO, TEXAS

Unified Development Code

STREET FEATURES AND ARRANGEMENTS. Historic districts and the downtown, as well as other distinct areas of the city have diverse character and any street furniture selected for these areas should complement these differences. In addition, the clustering of street furniture in one (1) place is recommended. Trash receptacles, seating, telephones and other street furniture should be grouped together.

A. CIRCULATION. A clear path-of-travel of thirty-six (36) inches wide shall be maintained in and around street features and arrangement.

B. SEATING. Seating should be physically comfortable and inviting, durable and attractive. Plaza and open space seating should also be socially comfortable by offering a variety of choices such as in the sun or shade, near traffic and activity or not, and alone or in groups.

C. DRINKING FOUNTAINS. Placing drinking fountains in new development is encouraged. Fountains should be placed within general areas of pedestrian traffic and located on accessible surfaces.

D. TRASH RECEPTACLES. Trash receptacles should blend visually with their surroundings and their design and location should make use as convenient as possible.

San Antonio, Tex., Unified Dev. Code art. VI, div. 4, §§ 35-646(a)(3)(A)–(D) (2009).

SAN DIEGO, CALIFORNIA

Planned Districts Chapter, Municipal Code

Within the Cass Street Commercial District, no alteration, construction, development or use of the abutting public right-of-way shall be permitted unless the streetscape and encroachment permit standards are met.

(2) BENCHES

(A) Materials

Benches located in the sidewalk right-of-way shall conform to one or more of the following materials: wood; wood and iron; wrought iron or cast iron; and formed iron.

(B) The siting of benches shall be as follows:

    (I) Benches shall not encroach into the required 8-foot sidewalk clearpath.

    (II) Benches shall not be located within 5 feet from the center of the sidewalk.

    (III) A bench located parallel to the sidewalk shall face the center of the sidewalk.

    (IV) If two or more benches are situated perpendicular to the sidewalk, the benches shall be sited to face each other.

(C) Advertisement on benches located in the public right-of-way shall be prohibited.

San Diego, Cal., Mun. Code ch. 15, art. 4, div. 4, §§ 154.0405 & (g)(2) (2009).

---

well as several control groups, researchers sought to understand the effects of converting streets into street parks on neighborhood social interactions. The results predictably showed significant increases in child-based activities on the street. Although adult interactions increased too, those tended to be in more formal, interior settings, not through casual contacts on the streets. The author's hypothesis for this surprising result is that "an environment designed for social activities may communicate to its occupants subtle norms about being social: it is perceived as a social arena affording socializing" (Skjaeveland 2001, p. 143).

The Project for Public Spaces, a New York–based nonprofit founded to expand on the work of William

H. Whyte, advocates an approach to street furniture referred to as *triangulation*. "Triangulation, when used as a technique for planning public spaces, means locating elements in a way that greatly increases the chances of activity occurring around them. The idea is to situate them so that the use of each builds off the other. For example, ... if a children's reading room in a new library is located adjacent to a playground in a park with a food kiosk, more activity will occur than if these facilities are sited separately" (Project for Public Spaces 2001, p. 63). So the use of street furniture to triangulate goes hand in hand with three other pedestrian-oriented features: (1) comfortable and safe places to wait,

(2) nearby parks and other public spaces, and
(3) attractive transit facilities.

Critics and admirers agree that street furniture can be overdone (Gibbons and Oberholzer 1992, pp. 3–4; Hedman 1984, pp. 95–97; M. Ryan 2000; Shaftoe 2008; Whyte 1988, p. 102). Keep street furniture simple; use few materials and coherent colors. To avoid visual clutter and pedestrian obstruction, consolidate street furniture at intervals along the street; these points will take on special significance as pedestrian rest stops. Toward the same ends, integrate signage with street furniture or integrate street furniture into building facades. Such practices are generally advocated in design manuals.

Coherent, Small-Scale Signage

IN TRADITIONAL CITIES, BUILDINGS DOMINATE STREETSCAPES owing to their relative size, strong vertical lines, and closeness to the street; landscaping and signage are secondary. In suburbs and suburb-like cities, roles are reversed. Buildings are so low, and are set back so far, that landscaping and signage become dominant image makers. The images created by suburban landscaping are generally positive, if a bit monotonous. The images created by signage are usually negative.

Local governments have responded to the proliferation of garish highway signs by regulating the number, types, and sizes of signs. Although avoiding the chaos of the commercial strip, the result of overzealous sign regulation can be almost as bad. Signs can cease to convey information effectively, which can have negative effects on local businesses, or to convey a sense of community character. They can be so standardized as to be tedious.

Some urban designers have recognized the creative possibilities afforded by good signage. If designed and applied thoughtfully, signs can add several pedestrian-oriented qualities to streetscapes: imageability, human scale, complexity, coherence, and, of course, legibility and wayfinding (see Fendley 2009).

In land development codes, the size limits of signs are usually related to lot frontage; the wider the lot, the bigger the sign or the more signs that may be displayed. A more rational basis for sizing signage is the design speed of the street where the signs are located. Along high-speed commuting routes, relatively large and

Signage scaled for speeding traffic. | *Edward T. McMahon*

FIGURE 5-2

Recommended Sign Specifications by Street Width and Vehicle Speed

Street Width	Speed (mph)	Letter Height (inches)	Total Area of Sign (square feet)[1]
Two lanes	15	4	6–8
Two lanes	30	7	18–25
Two lanes	45	10	36–50
Four lanes	30	9	28–40
Four lanes	45	13	64–90
Four lanes	60	17	106–150
Six lanes	30	9	70–100
Six lanes	45	14	70–100
Six lanes	60	19	134–190

Source: Ewald 1977, pp. 52–53.

1 The lower end of the range applies to institutional and residential areas; the upper end to commercial and industrial areas.

simple signs are required to convey a message quickly and conveniently to drivers. Conversely, on streets that are meant to be walkable and where design speeds are much lower, signs should be scaled down and made more interesting. Based on extensive study of traveler reaction times, the seminal work *Street Graphics* offers guidelines for sign area and letter height as a function of land use and travel speed. For streets with design speeds of 15 miles per hour, sign area should be limited to between six and eight square feet with four-inch lettering. These signs are ideal for walkable streets because the added complexity helps maintain pedestrians' interest in the streetscape (Ewald 1977, pp. 52–53; see also Mandelker 2004). The complete set of guidelines from *Street Graphics* is reproduced in figure 5-2.

In general, complexity is good, for it helps maintain pedestrian interest. But "high complexity urban areas must also be highly coherent" (Herzog, Kaplan, and Kaplan 1982, p. 58). The problem with a highway strip is not the surplus of information it imparts. Rather, it is the complete absence of structure to the information and its lack of relationship to the surrounding environment (Denis and Pontille 2010). Massive doses of unstructured information overwhelm. Incoherent, chaotic signage may even pose safety issues. Local governments have used traffic safety studies to justify street sign controls and the U.S. Supreme Court has upheld sign regulation in part on that basis.

As several visual preference studies have shown, including one study of street signage, scenes with moderate complexity, and high coherence, are most favored (Nasar 1987). Coherent signage has a consistent vocabulary of heights, sizes, shapes, materials, colors, and lettering. If signs have enough characteristics in common, the street scene will appear orderly, logical, and predictable to pedestrians strolling by. If not, it will

Complex but coherent streetscapes (Walnut Creek and Pasadena, California). | *Dan Burden*

appear messy. It is important to understand that signs need not, indeed should not, be identical in all respects, just similar in a few. Too much uniformity can render a streetscape devoid of character.

Finally, signs should convey a sense of place, either the place of business they advertise or the larger district in which the business is located (Ewald 1977). The best signs can do both. The most memorable places have memorable signage. In New Orleans, San Antonio, Hollywood, California, and other places whose character has made them pedestrian meccas, signs add to the fun and novelty of being there.

LOCAL CODE

EXAMPLES Signage

The code examples from San Diego and Nashville demonstrate two very different approaches to regulating the visual impact of signs. San Diego's code takes a highly detailed and prescriptive approach to signage, restricting the size and number of signs based on detailed numerical formulas. This approach provides less opportunity to allow a different but appealing sign but provides more clarity. One interesting aspect of San Diego's code is the requirement that *blade* (projecting) signs either take the shape of a graphic representation of the product or services offered or include such an image on the sign. This requirement encourages a certain look to blade signs without creating uniformity or restricting creativity. In contrast, Nashville's code provides a simple, discretionary standard for signs in neighborhood landmark districts, providing that a sign must fit a neighborhood's context and character in size and design. This approach is very flexible, but also very vague, providing little information to a business owner or community member regarding what might or might not be acceptable.

SAN DIEGO, CALIFORNIA | PLANNED DISTRICTS CHAPTER, MUNICIPAL CODE

Identification Signs

(A) Signs are permitted on the faces of each business establishment provided that no such sign shall project above the nearest parapet or eave of the building and signs parallel to the face of a building shall not project more than 12 inches from the building to which the signs are attached.

(B) One identification sign shall be permitted on the front or primary face of a business establishment. Said sign shall not exceed one square foot for each linear foot of frontage or 24 square feet, whichever is smaller, provided that said sign need not be less than 10 square feet in area.

(C) One identification sign on the side or rear wall of an establishment shall not exceed 16 square feet or one-half-square-foot for each linear foot of street or dedicated walkway frontage along those walls, whichever is smaller, provided that said sign need not be less than 8 square feet in area.

(D) One perpendicular (30 degrees or greater) projecting and/or hanging trade identification sign not to exceed 6 square feet per side shall be permitted on the front or primary face of each establishment provided however that the sign face is, either designed as a graphic representation of the goods or services provided at the particular establishment, e.g. a boot to advertise a shoe repair shop, or designed to include a graphic presentation on the sign.

(E) No free standing or roof top identifications signs shall be permitted with the following exceptions:

(I) For establishments located within arcade, court, office building or similar structure not fronting on the public right-of-way, a single free standing sign at the entrance to said court or arcade to identify the establishments within.

(II) Maximum height of such signs shall not exceed 4 feet above average adjacent natural grade.

(III) Maximum size for identification of each individual establishment shall not exceed 2.0 square feet for office and 3 square feet for retail.

(F) In lieu of a primary identification sign, 1 freestanding or hanging perpendicular sign, not to exceed 6 feet in height, with a total surface area on both sides not exceeding one-half the area of the permitted primary identification sign, shall be permitted. Only 1 such sign shall be permitted per establishment.

San Diego, Cal., Mun. Code ch. 15, art. 16, div. 4, § 1516.0403(b)(1) (2009).

NASHVILLE, TENNESSEE

Zoning Code

SIGNS. Any sign, where permitted as part of the neighborhood landmark development plan, shall be consistent with the context, scale, and character of the neighborhood and in particular streetscape where the district is located. The feature's mass and scale and the neighborhood in which it is located shall be considered in any sign size and design to ensure sensitivity and proportion to surrounding properties.

Nashville and Davidson County, Tenn., Code part II, tit. 17, ch. 17.40, art. IV, § 17.40.160(F)(4) (2009).

Special Pavement

CONCEIVING STREETS AS OUTDOOR ROOMS, the "walls" of the room are the buildings that bound and shape the street. The "ceiling" is the sky itself, which, if bordering buildings are roughly the same height and close together, will be perceived as a ceiling through the power of suggestion. The "floor" is the street and sidewalk surface. The degree to which these elements come together to create enclosed outdoor rooms can influence the degree and quality of neighborhood-level social interactions (Al-Homoud and Tassinary 2004; see also Talen 2000).

How important is the "floor"—its color, texture, and pattern—in making a street space feel more room-like? Arguing for its importance are the facts that the street and sidewalk surfaces are touched as well as seen, that a pedestrian's cone of vision is predominantly down-ward, and that surfaces seem more pedestrian scaled if textured. Special pavement can contribute something to at least four qualities of pedestrian-oriented design: human scale, complexity, coherence, and linkage.

Special paving's contribution is necessarily limited by the oblique angle at which pedestrians view pavement receding into the distance; any pattern quickly be-comes indiscernible. Bricks, cobbles, precast pavers, and patterned concrete cannot compensate for otherwise poorly defined street space. In at least one study, the complexity of paving patterns was negatively associated with residents' perceptions of their neighborhood (Zhang and Lin 2011), suggesting that care should be taken in applying this design element.

Moreover, special pavement is relatively expensive as streetscape improvements go. The cost of elaborate paving patterns might be better spent on elements such as tree planting that would have a greater impact both visually and with regard to improving comfort levels by providing shade.

Textured paving is probably best used as an accent rather than fill-in material, and used mainly where it serves some purpose other than a purely decorative one. Traffic calming is one such purpose. Used in a *gateway* entering a pedestrian zone, or in a crosswalk, the slight vibration caused by textured surfaces warns drivers to slow down and be on the lookout for pedes-trians (Dougald 2004; Ray 2008; Sandt 2011). Also, without costing a fortune, special pavement may be used to visually break up large paved areas; to provide linkage between buildings and streets, buildings and public spaces, or public spaces and one another; and to clearly separate pedestrian, bicycle, and motor vehicle rights-of-way where boundaries are less than obvious.

Special street and sidewalk treatments using brick pavers (Victoria, British Columbia; Greeley, Colorado). | *Dan Burden*

The most common use for textured pavements is, by far, in crosswalks. However, such surfaces may be less visible than normal striped crosswalks because they can blend into the surrounding road surface. To improve visibility, reflective lateral stripes can be added adjacent to the textured material (Ray 2008; Zegeer et al. 2002). Although if used in a crosswalk, wheelchair users and the visually impaired can find certain textured pave-

Use of textured surface for traffic calming and to delineate pedestrian space (Reston, Virginia; Santa Barbara, California). | *Adrienne Schmitz; Reid Ewing*

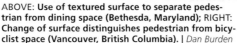

ABOVE: Use of textured surface to separate pedestrian from dining space (Bethesda, Maryland); RIGHT: Change of surface distinguishes pedestrian from bicyclist space (Vancouver, British Columbia). | *Dan Burden*

ments difficult to cross due to uneven settlement. The solution to this problem is to use interlocking concrete pavers since they do not settle unevenly.

Alternatively, colored concrete can be used effectively to improve pedestrian and bicyclist safety at a much lower cost than textured materials (Lin and Luo 2004). Paint should not be used to color concrete since it creates a slippery surface when wet. Instead, mineral oxide pigments can be mixed with concrete to create a range of color options. In Florida, Coral Gables and the city of South Miami use salmon-tinted concrete in their sidewalks.

Special Pavement

Aurora, Colorado's code focuses on special pavement for intersection and midblock crossings within transit-oriented development districts. The code sets out a hierarchy of pavement treatments depending on the proximity to the core of the district, the transit center. The code does not require use of colored paving and specially patterned pavers, but it suggests their possible use in the core and the area near the core. The code also notes that the presence of pedestrians and bicyclists should be another factor in determining the level of treatment. The Colorado Springs code provides for a patio or plaza area as one choice for developers for a required on-site public amenity. The code prohibits the use of asphalt for the plaza, requiring decorative pavers or textured and colored concrete.

AURORA, COLORADO | URBAN STREET STANDARDS

Pedestrian Crossing Treatments

A hierarchy of crossing treatments should be applied to intersection and mid-block crossings based on the location within the urban center or TOD [transit-oriented development] and the presence of pedestrians and bicyclists. When designing pedestrian crossings, appropriate signage and striping measures should be applied per the MUTCD (Manual on Uniform Traffic Control Devices). The hierarchy and appropriate locations include the following applications:

STANDARD MARKINGS—All crossings should be identified with parallel lines;
ENHANCED MARKINGS—Ladder striping should be added for crossings of streets in the edge and edge zone;
COLORED PAVING—A dark gray or other appropriate colors may be applied to the paving in crosswalks within core or transition zone;
SPECIAL PAVERS—A distinctly patterned paver may be applied to distinguish intersection crosswalks and mid-block crossings in the core or transition zone.

Aurora, Colo., Mun. Code § 126-36.5(V)(G)(2)(e) (2009).

COLORADO SPRINGS, COLORADO | MUNICIPAL CODE

Planning, Development and Building Chapter

A. Patio or plaza with seating areas, provided such patio or plaza has a minimum depth and width of ten feet (10'), and a minimum total area of three hundred (300) square feet.

1. Asphalt is prohibited as a paver; use of decorative pavers or textured, colored concrete is required.
2. Patios and plazas shall include pedestrian amenities intended to support these places as gathering areas.

Colorado Springs, Colo., Code § 7.4.1003(A) (2009).

Public Art

EVEN SPACES THAT ARE WELL DEFINED BY BUILDINGS or other vertical elements can be characterless and can lack a sense of place. Anecdotal evidence suggests that the introduction of art in public places can increase the level of pedestrian activity (Whyte 1988, p. 146). Public art has this power because of its ability to create a sense of place. Public art may not be essential for walkability, and may not even rank as highly desirable (given the many great streets without it), but it is a welcome addition.

Public art may contribute to several urban design qualities of streetscapes and public spaces, specifically, imageability, enclosure, human scale, complexity, and legibility. Public art can make associations with the past or the natural world, commemorate people and events, add decorative richness, and introduce whimsy and humor. All of these elements add to the imageability of places (McCarthy 2006).

If public art is sufficiently monumental, it can act as a landmark, as with Picasso's massive 50-foot-tall sculpture in Chicago's Daley Plaza and St. Louis's Gateway Arch. It can also overcome a fragmented frame of build-

ings that, by itself, cannot define a space. Most often, the art must have a vertical thrust to serve as a marker, and an open design to grasp and hold the space around it (Hedman 1984). This principle applies both to streets, whose end points can be marked with public art, and to parks and other public spaces, whose centers can be defined by public art.

Public art can humanize public spaces in subtle ways. In an impersonal world, public art represents a personal touch by the artist creating it and the institution erecting it. It can serve as a conversation piece and, in so doing, can cultivate social interaction among residents. It can also enliven often overlooked residual spaces—such as street medians, traffic circles, and parking lots—incorporating them into surrounding neighborhoods and providing connective elements that

reintegrate parts of streets and commercial districts (Winterbottom 2000).

Public art, in the form of murals on blank walls, can even create the illusion of transparency. A surprising number of blank sidewalls on urban buildings have windows and doors painted on them, an improvement over a blank wall but, of course, no substitute for the real thing.

Functional art can add detail and complexity to elements frequently passed over (Kroloff 1996). Artists designed street lamps with ribbons of steel and leaf cutouts to decorate the central business district in Mercer Island, Washington, whereas Santa Barbara, California, installed corn-themed streetlights in a new roundabout (Fleming 2007). Artistic bike racks are found in such cities as New York and Portland, Oregon, and "combine the utility of security with the aesthetics of art" (Martin 2008). Calgary, Alberta, has created a plan for integrating art into the extensive infrastructure used to collect and distribute water throughout the region. The plan's overall objective is to incorporate art that emphasizes the water's origins in the surrounding mountains and glaciers and helps communicate the need for greater conservation and efficiency at a time of shrinking supplies due to climate change (Garten 2009). Whether viewed as art or just quirky street furniture, these elements have the

Public art might depict associations with the past, or add decorative richness or whimsy (State College, Pennsylvania; Olympia, Washington; Chicago, Illinois). | *Dan Burden (left and center); Sam Newberg/Joe Urban (below)*

effect of individualizing space, which can increase its imageability.

Art does not have to be a painting or sculpture—it can be a live performance. In New York, live performances by musicians are scheduled to serenade subway passengers. In Los Angeles, the Metro system offers tours of its art, with volunteer guides describing the art, artists, and local community. The expansion of light-rail transit throughout U.S. metropolitan areas since the mid-1980s has also provided numerous opportunities for new public art at station platforms and other facilities, with many metropolitan areas adopting minimum-percentage-for-art policies as part of their transit capital programs (Banyas 2002). Public art has also been used to mitigate the effects of unsightly transportation elements, such as urban freeways, but with only modest success.

LOCAL CODE EXAMPLES

Public Art

Aurora's code requires every major development project within transit-oriented development districts to provide public art. The required art can include a sculpture or can consist of architectural elements in a building facade. Aurora also sets a minimum expenditure for the art and requires the submission of a public art plan. Minneapolis's code encourages developers to provide public art by providing floor/area ratio premiums as an incentive. To qualify, the art must meet or exceed a given value based on the capital cost of the principal structure in the development itself. The art must be highly visible to the public, and the developer is responsible for ongoing maintenance.

AURORA, COLORADO
Building and Zoning Code

1. PRINCIPLE. Art in public spaces and within private development that is visible from streets and public areas contributes to creating the identity of TODs [transit-oriented developments]. In this context, public art includes a wide variety of elements, ranging from free-standing artworks in parks to creative architectural elements incorporated into streetscapes and building facades. Art elements in differing materials, size, and subject matter should be incorporated throughout a TOD. A public art master plan that identifies themes and artwork placement is encouraged.

2. ART REQUIREMENT. Each development application for any development within the TOD district with a project valuation of $100,000 or more is required to provide public art. A public art plan shall be submitted along with the first site plan or contextual site plan for the development. . . . At the time of submittal, each applicant shall pay to the city a review fee in an amount established by the director of Library, Recreation, and Cultural Services in accordance with the provisions of section 2-587 of this code. The public art plan shall provide for the acquisition of outdoor works of art in compliance with the rules and regulations promulgated by the director of Library, Recreation, and Cultural Services.

3. MINIMUM EXPENDITURE. . . . The total minimum amount to be expended by the property owner on such art shall be calculated by multiplying the total project valuation included in any building permit application, by the amount of one percent.

Aurora, Colo., Building and Zoning Code ch. 146, art. 7, div. 6, § 146-728(K) (2009).

MINNEAPOLIS, MINNESOTA
Zoning Code

Public art, subject to the following standards:

A. The art shall be valued at not less than one-fourth (.25) of one (1) percent of the capital cost of the principal structure.

B. The art shall be located where it is highly visible to the public. If the art is located indoors, such space shall meet the minimum requirements for an indoor open space, interior through-block connection or skyway connecting corridor, as specified in this article.

C. The art shall be maintained in good order for the life of the principal structure.

Minneapolis, Minn., Code tit. 20, ch. 549, § 549.220(7) (2009).

Although public art can create unique and memorable places, it can do just the opposite without the appropriate investment of time and money. Creating public art master plans containing realistic budgets for maintenance is crucial for long-term success (Becker 2005; Ronit 2009). Planning for routine repair costs due to vandalism and everyday wear and tear will prevent public art from becoming an eyesore. Likewise, by investing resources in the public involvement process for art projects, cities can create a sense of community through these place-making projects (Blair, Pijawka, and Steiner 1998).

The next two features would rank higher if the question were, "What characteristics attract people to public spaces and cause them to linger there?" Water features and outdoor dining would probably be in the first tier. But the question instead is the more utilitarian, "What characteristics induce people to walk and use transit for their trip making?" When the question is asked that way, these two place-making features are apparently not as critical.

Water Features

THE PHRASE *SENSE OF PLACE* can be thought of as relating to the five senses. The more the senses are stimulated, the greater the sense of place. Water appeals to three senses—sight, hearing, and touch—and thus has unusual power as a place maker.

According to some researchers, the psychological and emotional values inherent in water make water features one of the most attractive design elements for parks and plazas (Russ 2002, p. 108), though that conclusion is not universally shared (Nordh, Alalouch, and Hartig 2011). These primal connections to the look, sound, and feel of water have led designers to place fountains and other water features in plazas and other important public spaces for centuries, and they have fostered the inclusion of water features into the urban design elements of scores of city general plans (see figure 5-3).

In some cases, water features are intended to be enjoyed solely by visual observation, with scale having an influence on the desired vantage point. Grand fountains, such as Buckingham Fountain in Chicago's Grant Park, are meant to be enjoyed at a distance. Others are

Water feature in Paley Park masks the sound of nearby conversations (New York, New York). | *Dan Burden*

FIGURE 5-3

Samples of Urban Design Policies That Incorporate Water Features

Jurisdiction	Source	Policy
Bellevue, Washington	Comprehensive Plan Policy UD-13	Encourage water as an auditory and tactile design element in both the built and natural environment. In the built environment, such features should be designed to minimize water loss and be required to utilize recirculating or recycled water.
Dallas, Texas	Forward Dallas Comprehensive Plan	Pedestrian plazas and green open space offer interesting public places for people to enjoy the street experience. These should incorporate water features, sculptures, art, or other architectural objects or focal points.
West Jordan, Utah	Downtown Revitalization Plan, Urban Design Element Policy 2	Water features should be placed in certain locations, both as a draw and to reflect the historic role of water in the valley.

Water features appeal to sight, sound, and touch (Boston, Massachusetts; Berlin, Germany). | *Boston Natural Areas Network; Reid Ewing*

designed to be intimate and to invite close inspection.

A central part of the design process is determining whether the water will be still or moving: "Moving water gives a sense of life. Still water conveys unity and rest and may be used to clarify a plan" (Lynch 1971, p.

211; see also Nasar and Lin 2003). Still water also acts as a mirror to reflect the sun, sky, or a particular structure, as with the Lincoln Memorial Reflecting Pool on the National Mall, whereas moving water creates *white noise* that many find soothing and refreshing (Carmona et al. 2003, p. 111; Loukaitou-Sideris and Banerjee 1998, p. 193).

Moving water can help mask the sounds of nearby conversations—as William H. Whyte (1988) discovered in New York's Paley Park—aurally providing a measure of privacy even in a crowded space. In fact, Amanda Burden

LOCAL CODE

EXAMPLES Water Features

Zoning codes increasingly encourage water features as a pleasant option in pedestrian-oriented areas. Louisville, Kentucky's code sets out an expectation that new or improved open spaces within the downtown area will contain a fountain or water feature among other pedestrian-friendly elements. Pasadena, California's code encourages fountains by requiring new projects within a certain district to include at least one "craftsmanship element" and two "building elements," and it includes fountains among the choices for each.

LOUISVILLE, KENTUCKY
Land Development Code

Any newly developed or improved open space accessible to the public should generally:

1. Create a comfortable and interesting place to rest.
2. Let people clearly know it's there and that it's accessible.
3. Provide plenty of seating (about one linear foot for every 30 square feet of paved open space.
4. Have enough lighting to create a safe nighttime environment.
5. Use fountains or other water features.
6. Incorporate public art.

Louisville, Ky., Land Dev. Code § 3.3B.B.12 (2009).

PASADENA, CALIFORNIA
Zoning Code

CRAFTSMANSHIP ELEMENT. Each project shall incorporate into the design at least one feature such as iron grates, tile fountains, cast terra cotta, wood work, stenciled ornament or other elements as approved by the Design Review authority.

BUILDING ELEMENT. In addition to the above requirements, each new project shall incorporate at least two building elements. Building elements include: upper floor loggias, roofed balconies supported by brackets or by columns at the ground floor, exterior wooden or masonry stairs with closed risers, or tile or masonry fountain.

Pasadena, Cal., Zoning Code s. 17.22.080(E) (2012).

The Canalscape design project envisions the use of existing canals as urban amenities for the city of Phoenix, Arizona. | *Canalscape*

(1977) observes that when the waterfall at New York's Greenacre Park is abruptly turned off, people cut short their conversations and prepare to depart: "The sounds of the city suddenly fill the park, absorbing it and transforming an oasis into an adjunct of the street" (p. 33).

The masking properties of moving water can also be used to help mitigate the negative effects of urban noise sources. In Las Vegas, a falling water feature was included in the Lewis Avenue Corridor project to help improve the quality of the central plaza by buffering pedestrians from the sounds of nearby auto traffic (Jost 2007).

Some water features perform multiple functions. Portland, Oregon's Jamison Square Park in the Pearl District contains a stepped stone wall fountain that, when the water is turned off, becomes a performance amphitheater (Hazelrigg 2006). The *Benson Bubbler* drinking fountains, also in Portland, not only provide drinking

water and a delightful street design element, they also serve as an icon for the city and are incorporated into the logo for the city's water bureau.

In some cases, the water feature is already present, and it is the surrounding development that reorients to leverage the feature's proximity into a central design element. Examples of this approach come from the Canalscape projects sprouting up around the Arizona Canal in Phoenix (Ellin 2010; Ewan 2002).

Outdoor Dining

OUTDOOR DINING RIVALS WATER IN ITS APPEAL TO THE SENSES, arguably even surpassing water by adding smell and (for those dining) taste. In our urban design qualities study, outdoor dining was a contributor to three valued qualities of streetscapes: imageability, complexity, and linkage (Ewing and Handy 2009). Only the number of people on the street had as extensive an effect on perceived qualities.

From restaurant seating and outdoor cafés to street vendors and food trucks, outdoor dining is nearly unmatched in creating an active and lively street environment. "If you want to seed a place with activity, put out food," William H. Whyte (1980) writes. "In New York, at every plaza or set of steps with a lively social life, you will almost invariably find a food vendor at the corner and a knot of people around him—eating, schmoozing, or just standing" (p. 50). As some have pointed out, this clustering is just the outdoor analog of what people frequently observe at indoor parties—everyone ends up in the kitchen. The issue is fundamentally one of hospitality. As with seating, providing food in a public setting

gives a sense of comfort and entices people to linger, which enlivens the space.

In a symbiotic way, as people are attracted by the food, more people are drawn by the presence of the initial crowd (Montgomery 1997). At some point, untangling who is the audience from who is the show becomes difficult. David Engwicht (1993) notes that the seats of the outdoor cafés in Paris are not arranged around all sides of the table, but are all on the building side, facing out to the street. "The … scene illustrates perfectly the centuries old European tradition of the street as a stage—the social and cultural epicenter of urban living" (p. 16). For the pedestrian, the mere presence of people dining at outdoor

Outdoor dining can be anything from a couple of tables outside a coffee shop to a designated space with full restaurant service (Boulder, Colorado; Edmonton, Alberta). | *City of Boulder, Colorado; Dan Burden*

cafés can promote the passive contacts that are such an important part of the sidewalk's role in social activity, while the outdoor seating facilitates the observation of the street's exchange of goods, services, and information. In these ways, according to David Sucher (2003), outdoor dining contributes to one of the main purposes of cities, which is bumping into people.

Cafés can also provide a softening of building edges. If buildings are the walls of an outdoor room, then café seating provides the furniture that helps break up the monotony and hardness of those walls. It also helps blur the distinction between the indoors and the outdoors, both functionally and psychologically (Gehl, Kaefer, and Reigstad 2006). This indistinctness helps provide a smooth transition between spaces, adding to that notion of the *building giving to the street* discussed in chapter 3. Plantings, coverings, shade, and color enhance the outdoor dining areas, as well as the pedestrian environment, while the outdoor dining helps keep the sidewalk lively after dark.

In a new twist, street food stalls are now being used in some cities to screen the edges of surface parking lots (Rodgers and Roy 2010). In downtown Portland, Oregon, for example, food carts have become so abundant that the parking lot behind the row of vendors has become completely obscured. The popularity of food trucks has escalated rapidly in recent years. Food

TOP: **Outdoor food vendors (New York, New York);** ABOVE: **Blurring the distinction between indoor and outdoor spaces (Victoria, British Columbia).** | *Dan Burden*

EXAMPLES Outdoor Dining

San Diego, California, and Montgomery, Alabama, take two different approaches to enlivening the pedestrian environment through outdoor eating. San Diego's code does so by permitting sidewalk cafés within indicated zones. Sidewalk café furnishings must be movable or affixed to adjacent buildings. The decision to allow a sidewalk café in a given location is discretionary; major factors in the determination include the effect on pedestrians' right-of-way and the ability of the café to make the area more attractive to pedestrians and to increase pedestrian traffic.

Montgomery's zoning code allows sidewalk food vendors. Having found that "vending on the public sidewalks promotes the public convenience by contributing to an active and attractive pedestrian environment," the code creates a specified vending district wherein vending is permitted, requires vendors to be licensed, and restricts sales to food and nonalcoholic beverages.

SAN DIEGO, CALIFORNIA

Municipal Code

SIDEWALK CAFES. Sidewalk cafes may be permitted with a Neighborhood Use Permit in the zones indicated with an "N" in the Use Regulations Tables in Chapter 13, Article 1 (Base Zones) subject to the provisions of this section.

(A) The decision maker will evaluate the following to determine if a sidewalk cafe is a suitable use for the proposed site and will not infringe on the use of the *public right-of-way* by pedestrians:

    (1) The width of the sidewalk;

    (2) The design and relationship of the cafe to other existing or planned uses in the vicinity;

    (3) The amount of pedestrian use and the impact of the cafe's location on pedestrian activity; and

    (4) The ability of the cafe to fit the character of the area, create an outdoor pedestrian plaza, intensify pedestrian activity, and make the *street* activity more attractive.

(I) The furnishings of the interior of a sidewalk cafe shall consist solely of moveable tables, moveable chairs, and moveable umbrellas. Landscaping may be placed in moveable planters or planted in the ground inside the delineated cafe area adjacent to the barrier. Lighting fixtures may be permanently affixed to the front of the main building.

San Diego, Cal., Mun. Code ch. 14, art. 1, div. 6, §§141.0621 (2009).

MONTGOMERY, ALABAMA

Zoning Code

For the purpose of this ordinance the City Council does hereby create a Vending District to permit sidewalk vending.

A) Vending district means the zone or area specifically designated for sidewalk vending.

B) Cart means any portable vending device, pushcart, or any other wheeled vehicle or device which may be moved without the assistance of a motor and which is not required to be licensed and registered by the Department of Motor Vehicles, used for the displaying, storing or transporting of articles offered for sale by a vendor, and which does not exceed four feet in width, six feet in length, excluding trailer hitch or handle bars, and five feet in height, excluding canopy or cover. A cart that is towable by means of a trailer hitch is permitted provided it does not exceed the aforementioned size limits.

PERMITTED MERCHANDISE. No merchandise shall be sold by a vendor from a cart in a vending district except the merchandise approved. Permitted merchandise shall be limited to food and nonalcoholic beverages. . . .

Montgomery, Ala., Code app. C, art. VI, § 10.14.1 (2007).

---

trucks, often with gourmet offerings, congregate at specified locations, generally at lunchtime, drawing office workers and others to purchase and eat lunch in a park or makeshift picnic area. In Phoenix, Arizona, a weekly event draws about a dozen different trucks to an unused parking lot. Tables and canopies are set up, and bands entertain the lunchtime crowd. In both cases, food trucks and stalls animate otherwise underused street and sidewalk space, drawing people into former dead spaces.

Food vendors can also provide a security function (Barnett 2003, p. 235). Although they operate in publicly owned spaces, the providers of food, be they cart vendors or café purveyors, exercise informal dominion over the areas that their equipment and furniture occupy; they have a sense of responsibility for the surrounding territory as well. Probably no one has more attentive eyes on the street than a café waiter or a hotdog vendor. They are the "mayors" of their territories (Whyte 1980, p. 64), and it is in their interest to see that the spaces are safe and reasonably orderly.

Informal examples of outdoor dining are seen throughout New York City. A simple kiosk dispensing French street food at First Park makes it a popular neighborhood gathering space. The New York Public Library provides a series of well-designed spaces for sitting, reading, and eating. Steps, nooks, and plenty of public tables and chairs create seating for patrons and a connection to the street environment. Nearby Bryant Park provides kiosks that offer coffee and light meals, as well as nearly 1,000 lightweight chairs that can be moved throughout the park for improvised outdoor dining opportunities. In Salt Lake City, Utah, a popular Italian bistro uses (with the city's permission) an adjacent park for outdoor dining, thereby turning a fenced-in space known for its drug dealing (similar to Bryant Park before its renovation) into a safe, vibrant pocket park.

As shown through these examples, many cities—as well as suburban town centers—now embrace various kinds of outdoor dining. It is important to note that outdoor dining need not be large scale to be effective. Some of the most charming outdoor settings are created when cafés and coffee shops put out two or three small tables and a few chairs on the sidewalk. They should be encouraged, not prohibited.

Underground Utilities

IN MOST EUROPEAN COUNTRIES, utility lines are routinely placed underground, primarily to prevent collisions of vehicles with utility poles (FHWA 2001). In the United States, utilities are primarily carried on overhead utility lines. When they are relocated underground, it is for aesthetic rather than safety or institutional reasons. Our main-street visual preference survey found underground utilities, along with the quality of pavement maintenance, to be significant determinants of preference (Ewing et al. 2005). They were included to control for purely aesthetic effects.

Underground utilities eliminate the need for most tree trimming, reduce some electrical hazards, and nearly eliminate the need for extensive restoration efforts after major storms (FHWA 2001). In response to the 2004 and 2005 hurricanes, the Florida Public Service Commission (FPSC 2007) recommended that all utilities in the state be moved underground as a means of storm hardening.

The benefits of relocation as a traffic safety countermeasure are also clear (Lacy et al. 2004). Because of the structural strength and small impact area of utility poles, vehicle crashes tend to be severe. Nearly 40 percent of utility pole crashes involve some type of injury. Street trees are the only object type more frequently struck in fatal fixed-object crashes. Because of their enclosure of street space, trees may actually reduce crash rates in urban settings. Moreover, trees create a more attractive environment for pedestrians, whereas utility poles do not.

Visual impact of overhead utilities versus trees and buried lines. |
Michael King

Underground Utilities

Both Palo Alto, California, and Flagstaff, Arizona, encourage locating utilities underground. Palo Alto's code requires underground utility location for all new construction, but it provides flexibility where infeasible or impractical by allowing the director of utilities the discretion to allow exceptions. Flagstaff's provisions, found in the city's design standards, require all utilities in certain neighborhoods to be located underground and also encourage their location in rear alleys so that access and utility boxes are also hidden from view.

PALO ALTO, CALIFORNIA
Municipal Code

The council finds and determines that the public interest requires that all poles, overhead lines and associated overhead structures used in supplying electric service, communications service or similar associated service to be constructed in the city of Palo Alto after July 1, 1965, shall be placed in underground locations in order to promote and preserve the health, safety and general welfare of the public and to assure the orderly development of the city of Palo Alto. The director of utilities, or designee, may authorize poles, overhead lines and associated overhead structures for new construction when the director determines that an installation in an underground location in any particular instance would not be feasible or practicable. The decision of the director is final.

Palo Alto, Cal., Mun. Code § 12.16.010 (2009).

FLAGSTAFF, ARIZONA | DESIGN STANDARDS
Utility Placement in Thoroughfares

In Traditional Neighborhood developments all utilities shall be located underground in compliance with the following standards.
. . . Electric, telephone, cable and gas utilities ("dry" utilities) shall be located in Alleys or Lanes where these are provided to minimize above ground utility meters and boxes in the front of the property.

Flagstaff, Ariz., Engineering Design and Construction Standards and Specifications, 10-12-015.1. (2009).

Despite these functional and aesthetic benefits, the undergrounding of utilities is seldom addressed in TOD and street design manuals. An exception is Charlotte, North Carolina's *Urban Street Design Guidelines*. The guidelines call for placing utilities underground, wherever feasible, "To preserve sidewalk capacity for pedestrians, maintain a clear zone per ADA [Americans with Disabilities Act] requirements, and allow larger trees and other aesthetic treatments" (thereby enhancing the pedestrian nature of these streets). The guidelines say that if underground placement is not feasible, the next most preferable location is at the back of property. If poles must be located along the street frontage, they should be placed in the sidewalk amenity zone. Under no circumstances should they be placed in the sidewalk. Utility poles should be consolidated where possible, with redundant poles

removed in retrofit situations (Charlotte Department of Transportation 2007, p. 72).

The high cost associated with burying existing utility lines is recognized by some guides. Targeting areas most likely to benefit from the treatment is more cost-effective than attempting to relocate all lines within a jurisdiction.

In some cities where underground space has become crowded with utilities and other infrastructure, utility planners are moving toward the use of *utilidors*—joint-use underground tunnels that can contain multiple utilities, including the traditional overhead types (electricity and telephone), as well as water, sewerage, gas, and fiber optics. Although such facilities have obvious operational advantages, their higher initial cost and associated institutional and legal complexities limit their practicality to central business districts and large master-planned developments.

The elements outlined in this chapter, standing alone, would probably do very little to improve overall pedestrian friendliness. When combined with the other, more central elements described in earlier chapters, however, these traits can work to increase visual complexity and character and thereby improve overall imageability. And with increased imageability comes greater attraction and use.

CHAPTER 6

CONCLUSION

IT HAS BEEN SAID THAT URBAN DESIGN is the part of the built environment most overlooked by the professions: with architects focused primarily on structures and planners mainly on infrastructure, no one is charged with paying attention to the fine-grained, human-scaled features that can make or break the success of places. This claim, of course, is not completely accurate. Many excellent urban spaces (some of which are featured in the pages of this book) were designed by architects and planners. But there is still ample room for improvement in the design of much of metropolitan America.

The truth of this assertion is illustrated by the experience of a developer in Salt Lake City who would occasionally present slide shows to city councils and planning commissions. Many of his slides depicted commercial strips devoid of charm and pedestrians. The reaction of city councilors and planning commissioners was nearly always one of disgust. In response, the developer would challenge his audience to identify the common thread running through the slides. After allowing a few guesses, he would tell them: "The design of each of these street environments was allowed by your zoning code; in many cases, the code required it."

Fortunately, the content of local codes is beginning to change. Walsh (2012) reports on 42 localities that have recently adopted major overhauls to their codes, altering public right-of-way and geometric standards, urban design guidelines, and planning and development regulations to improve the pedestrian environment. In many cases, those revisions have been driven by citizen demand, not city staff. In Amarillo, Texas, the citizen-led Downtown Development Committee pushed for the creation of new urban design standards that would foster a more walkable and active downtown district. The resulting standards, adopted in 2010, integrate many of the features addressed in this book, setting sidewalk width, lighting, street connectivity, building edge, and street tree and street furniture standards to optimize pedestrian scale and comfort. Popular support for these standards was demonstrated when 70 percent of the public voted against a 2011 referendum that would have repealed them.

The city of Big Lake, Minnesota, followed a slightly different path but achieved similar results. Big Lake first adopted a series of voluntary design guidelines for its downtown district in 2004, addressing such topics as building orientation, lighting, signage, materials, and public space design. A year

New design standards have made downtown Amarillo, Texas, more pedestrian friendly. | *Melissa Dailey*

later, support for the guidelines led the city to convert them into mandatory standards implemented through a downtown overlay zone. In 2008, the city created a new transitional zone, adjacent to downtown, where the design standards are treated as guidelines. To facilitate the differing applications of the standards—mandatory in downtown, advisory in the transition zone—the city itemizes the overall design elements (such as parking, building placement, or open space), and then provides the related

guidelines (often illustrated with photos and sketches) and associated regulations.

Another example is *Miami 21*, the form-based code adopted by the city of Miami, Florida, in 2010. Guided by the principles of new urbanism and smart growth, the code favors infill development, encourages development at transit stops, and emphasizes mixed uses, concealed parking, and ground-level activity, all in an effort to improve the pedestrian environment.

LOCAL CODE

EXAMPLES ## Building Edge Standards

AMARILLO, TEXAS

- Buildings shall face the street or other public spaces with a setback of no more than five feet from the back of the city right-of-way.

- Changes to existing building facades shall be consistent with existing architecture, architectural features, and floor plans. The ground level shall be designed to allow conversion to retail or other active uses if they are not feasible at the time of opening.

- Street-facing facades shall have significant transparency with windows.

- Overly tinted, reflective, or opaque glass is not allowed on the ground floor of buildings.

- The ground floor of buildings shall include architectural relief at least every 30 feet. This relief may include, but is not limited to, doors, change in depth, columns or post, windows, and changes in materials.

- New buildings should differentiate between the first and second floors.

- Windows, stoops, and porches shall open to the street.

- Primary building entrances shall be clearly articulated using elements such as awnings, canopies, recessed entry, or other similar treatments.

- Corner entrances are encouraged for strong visibility at intersections.

- Long facades shall be broken up with articulation or other architectural treatments.

- Where office and retail/entertainment spaces coexist, consideration should be given to placing the retail entrances and prime exposure at the corners and the office entrances at midblock locations.

- Bringing restaurant and retail activities out to the walkway is strongly encouraged where unobstructed pedestrian walkway is maintained.

- Operable windows are encouraged for all buildings.

Source: Amarillo, Tex., Downtown Amarillo Urban Design Standards, p. 14 (2010).

Summary

IF EVER THERE WERE A TIME FOR CHANGE in how we design urban space, now would be that time. With the challenges of climate change and other environmental limits calling for a reduction in auto travel, rising gas prices and the prospects of *peak oil* providing financial incentive to increase walking and bicycling, and growing concerns about public health and the need for more active lifestyles, the call for well-designed pedestrian- and transit-oriented spaces has never been greater. And consumer demand for such places has never been higher. As outlined in the introduction to this book, market preference for pedestrian-oriented urban environments is growing in the United States—making up more than half the market, by some estimates—and that will only increase as baby boomers age and millennials enter the market. These shifts are already apparent in real estate prices, with consumer demand for pedestrian-oriented communities leading to significant price premiums.

The purpose of this book is to provide a how-to guide for bridging the gap between the sprawled streetscapes that are typical of many cities and towns and the urban environments being sought by so many Americans. The book attempts to operationalize a half-century of theories about urban design in ways that are meaningful and useful to the thousands of people—planners, planning commissioners, city council members, developers, and citizens—who are seeking to build better, more livable environments. Through a

LEFT: **Initial design for a proposed gas station (Big Lake, Minnesota); ABOVE: The revised design in response to the city's design standards (Big Lake, Minnesota).** | *Holiday*

structured set of checklists, this volume provides guidance on the design features the authors have observed as being the most important in creating successful pedestrian-oriented places. These recommendations may not appeal to everyone, but they provide a basis for discussion about the urban environment and how to make it more sustainable and livable.

Miami 21 is a holistic approach to land use and urban planning. It seeks to enhance the public realm with more active and inviting streets. Mixed-use areas should provide retail and services within walking distance of all neighborhoods. Entrances should be located to promote pedestrians' use of the sidewalk rather than to accommodate vehicle access. Ten-foot setbacks in such areas provide additional sidewalk space (Miami, Florida). | *James Wassell*

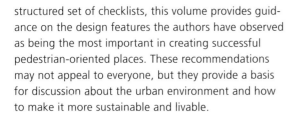

Example of Streetscape/Site Planning Elements

BIG LAKE, MINNESOTA

Parking Guidelines

- Off-street parking should not be located between a building and the street or main road it faces. Parking should be distributed around the building, especially to the side and back. Shared parking should be encouraged to take advantage of varying parking demands between mixed uses.

- Where a parking lot is located along a street, it should be well landscaped and screened with a combination of fencing or wall plantings along the street edge. Larger parking areas should be planned with internal landscaping and divided into smaller areas where possible.

- Opportunities for several smaller parking areas should be sought. Quantity should be balanced with aesthetics to avoid views of vast parking lots.

- On-street parking is encouraged on downtown streets. Streets should be designed with the parking zone designated either by curbing or with a change in paving materials. Where possible, shared access and parking should be encouraged.

Parking Regulations

- All off-street parking areas shall be screened in accordance with the applicable provisions of the Big Lake Zoning Ordinance.

- Where a parking lot is located along a street, it shall be well landscaped and screened with a combination of fencing or wall plantings along the street edge.

- Parking areas of more than 30 spaces shall include planting islands equivalent to 15 percent of the total area. No parking area planting island shall have any dimension (length or width) of less than ten feet.

- Existing parking areas not in conformance with this regulation shall be brought into compliance with the screening requirements in conjunction with any permit or other activity that is subject to these standards.

Source: Big Lake, Minn., Downtown Design Standards, p. 15 (2008).

References

1000 Friends of Oregon. 1993. *Making the Land Use, Transportation, Air Quality Connection: The Pedestrian Environment*. Portland: 1000 Friends of Oregon.

AASHTO (American Association of State Highway and Transportation Officials). 2004a. *A Guide for Achieving Flexibility in Highway Design*. Washington, DC: AASHTO.

———. 2004b. *A Policy on Geometric Design of Highways and Streets*. 4th ed. Washington DC: AASHTO.

———. 2005. *Roadway Lighting Design Guide*. Washington, DC: AASHTO.

Abramson, D.B. 2008. "Haussmann and Le Corbusier in China: Land Control and the Design of Streets in Urban Redevelopment." *Journal of Urban Design* 13 (2): 231–56.

Acharya, G., and L.L. Bennett. 2001. "Valuing Open Space and Land-Use Patterns in Urban Watersheds." *Journal of Real Estate Finance and Economics* 33 (2): 221–37.

Agrawal, A., and P. Schimek. 2007. "Extent and Correlates of Walking in the USA." *Transportation Research Part D* 12 (8): 548–63.

Agrawal, A., M. Schlossberg, and K. Irvin. 2008. "How Far, by Which Route, and Why? A Spatial Analysis of Pedestrian Preference." *Journal of Urban Design* 13 (1): 81–98.

AIA (American Institute of Architects). 2006. "Strengthening Oklahoma City One Bus Stop at a Time." Unpublished.

Alexander, C., S. Ishikawa, and M. Silverstein. 1977. *A Pattern Language: Towns, Buildings, Construction*. New York: Oxford University Press.

Al-Homoud, M., and L.G. Tassinary. 2004. "Social Interactions at the Neighborhood-Level as a Function of External Space Enclosure." *Journal of Architectural and Planning Research* 21 (1): 10–23.

Anderson, S.T., and S.E. West. 2006. "Open Space, Residential Property Values, and Spatial Context." *Regional Science and Urban Economics* 36 (6): 773–89.

Appleyard, D. 1981. *Livable Streets*. Berkeley: University of California Press.

Arnold, H. 1993. *Trees in Urban Design*. New York: Van Nostrand Reinhold.

Ayerdi-Kaplan, M., and F.W. Clarke. 2011. "Transbay Transit Center Art Program: Transformative Power of Public Art—The Role of Art in San Francisco's Transbay Transit Center." Paper presented at the 90th Annual Meeting of the Transportation Research Board, Washington, DC, January 23–27.

Bacon, E. 1974. *Design of Cities*. New York: Viking Press.

Bailey, L. 2004. *Aging Americans: Stranded without Options*. Washington, DC: Surface Transportation Policy Project.

Banyas, R. 2002. "The Transit Landscape." *Public Art Review* 13 (2): 10–16.

Barnett, J. 2003. *Redesigning Cities: Principles, Practice, Implementation*. Chicago: Planners Press.

Bartholomew, K. 1995. *Policies & Places: Land Use and Transport in the United Kingdom and the Netherlands*. Portland, OR: 1000 Friends of Oregon.

Bayer, A., and L. Harper. 2000. *Fixing to Stay: A National Survey of Housing and Home Modification Issues*. Washington, DC: AARP.

Beaumont, C., and L. Tucker. 2002. "Big-Box Sprawl and How to Control It." *Municipal Lawyer* 43 (2): 6–9, 30–31.

Becker, J. 2005. "Plan, Plan, Plan, Do." *Public Art Review* 15 (2): 5.

Belden Russonello & Stewart. 2003. *Americans' Attitudes toward Walking and Creating Better Walking Communities*. Washington, DC: Surface Transportation Policy Project.

———. 2004. *National Survey on Communities*. Washington, DC: National Association of Realtors and Smart Growth America.

———. 2011. *The 2011 Community Preference Survey: What Americans Are Looking for When Deciding Where to Live*. Washington, DC: National Association of Realtors.

Belmont, S. 2002. *Cities in Full: Recognizing and Realizing the Great Potential of Urban America*. Chicago: American Planning Association.

Blair, J.M., K.D. Pijawka, and F. Steiner. 1998. "Public Art in Mitigation Planning." *Journal of the American Planning Association* 64 (2): 221–35.

Blumenfeld, E., and T. Yatzeck. 1996. "Public Transportation as Collaborative Art: MetroLink, St. Louis." *Transportation Research Record* 1549: 79–84.

Blumenfeld, H. 1967. *The Modern Metropolis: Its Origins, Growth, Characteristics, and Planning*. Cambridge, MA: MIT Press.

Boarnet, M.G., and R. Crane. 2001. "The Influence of Land Use on Travel Behavior: Specification and Estimation Strategies." *Transportation Research A* 35 (9): 823–45.

Boarnet, M.G., K. Day, C. Anderson, T. McMillan, and M. Alfonzo. 2005. "California's Safe Routes to School Program: Impacts on Walking, Bicycling, and Pedestrian Safety." *Journal of the American Planning Association* 71 (3): 301–17.

Boarnet, M.G., and M. Greenwald. 2000. "Land Use, Urban Design, and Non-Work Travel: Reproducing for Portland, Oregon Empirical Tests from Other Urban Areas." *Transportation Research Record* 1722: 27–37.

Boarnet, M.G., K.S. Nesamani, and C. Scott Smith. 2004. "Comparing the Influence of Land Use on Nonwork Trip Generation and Vehicle Distance Traveled: An Analysis Using Travel Diary Data." Paper presented at the 83rd Annual Meeting of the Transportation Research Board, Washington DC, January 11–15.

Boarnet, M.G., and S. Sarmiento. 1998. "Can Land-Use Policy Really Affect Travel Behavior? A Study of the Link between Non-Work Travel and Land-Use Characteristics." *Urban Studies* 35 (7): 1155–69.

Bodmer, L.A., and M.A. Reiner. 1977. "Approach to the Planning and Design of Transit Shelters." *Transportation Research Record* 625: 48–53.

Bohl, C.C. 2002. *Place Making: Developing Town Centers, Main Streets, and Urban Villages*. Washington, DC: Urban Land Institute.

Bowman, B.L., and R.L. Vecellio. 1994. "The Effect of Urban/Suburban Median Types on Both Vehicular and Pedestrian Safety." *Transportation Research Record* 1445: 169–79.

Bressi, T.W. 1995. "New York Holds the Trump Card." *Planning* 61 (5): 4–10.

Brown, G.Z. 1985. *Sun, Wind, and Light: Architectural Design Strategies*. New York: John Wiley & Sons.

Burden, A. 1977. *Greenacre Park*. New York: Project for Public Spaces.

Burden, D., and P. Lagerway. 1999. "Road Diets: Fixing the Big Roads." Walkable Communities Inc. http://www.walkable.org/assets/downloads/roaddiets.pdf.

Calthorpe, P. 1993. *The Next American Metropolis: Ecology, Community, and the American Dream*. New York: Princeton Architectural Press.

Campo, D., and B.D. Ryan. 2008. "The Entertainment Zone: Unplanned Nightlife and the Revitalization of the American Downtown." *Journal of Urban Design* 13 (3): 291–315.

Campoli, J., and A.S. MacLean. 2007. *Visualizing Density*. Cambridge, MA: Lincoln Institute of Land Policy.

Capella, J. 1998. "Sitting Outdoors." *Domus*, March, p. 46.

Capital Area Transportation Authority. 2011. *Designing for Transit-Oriented Development in Greater Lansing*. Lansing, MI: CATA.

Cappe, L. 1991. "Including Transit." In *Public Streets for Public Use*, ed. A.V. Moudon, pp. 290–98. New York: Columbia University Press.

Carmona, M., T. Heath, T. Oc, and S. Tiesdell. 2003. *Public Places: Urban Spaces*. Oxford, UK: Architectural Press.

Center for Neighborhood Technology. 2011. *Literature Review: Statistical Methods*. Seattle: King County Metro Transit.

Cervero, R. 1994. "Transit-Based Housing in California: Evidence on Ridership Impacts." *Transport Policy* 1 (3): 174–83.

———. 2003. "The Built Environment and Travel: Evidence from the United States." *European Journal of Transport and Infrastructure Research* 3 (2): 119–37.

Cervero, R., A. Adkins, and C. Sullivan. 2009. "Are TODs Over-Parked?" UCTC Research Paper no. 882, University of California, Berkeley.

Cervero, R., and P. Bosselmann. 1998. "Transit Villages: Assessing the Market Potential through Visual Simulation." *Journal of Architectural and Planning Research* 15 (3): 181–96.

Cervero, R., C. Ferrell, and S. Murphy. 2002. "Transit-Oriented Development and Joint Development in the United States: A Literature Review." TCRP Report no. 52, Transit Cooperative Research Program, Washington, DC.

Charlotte Department of Transportation. 2007. *Urban Street Design Guidelines*. Charlotte, NC: Charlotte Department of Transportation.

Chen, L., C. Chen, and R. Ewing. 2012. "The Relative Effectiveness of Pedestrian Safety Countermeasures at Urban Intersections: Lessons from a New York City Experience." Paper presented at the 91st Annual Meeting of the Transportation Research Board, Washington, DC, January 22–26. http://docs.trb.org/prp/12-3237.pdf.

Childs, M.C. 2001. "Civic Ecosystems." *Journal of Urban Design* 6 (1): 55–72.

———. 2009. "Civic Concinnity." *Journal of Urban Design* 14 (2): 131–45.

Chu, X., M. Guttenplan, and A. Kourtellis. 2007. "Considering Usage and Safety Effects in Guidelines for Uncontrolled Midblock Crosswalks." *TRB 86th Annual Meeting Compendium of Papers*. Washington, DC: Transportation Research Board. CD-ROM.

City of Amarillo. 2010. *Downtown Amarillo Urban Design Standards*. Amarillo, TX: City of Amarillo.

City of Austin. 2006. *Transit-Oriented Development Guidebook*. Austin, TX: City of Austin.

City of Big Lake. 2008. *Downtown Design Standards*. Big Lake, MN: City of Big Lake.

City of Fresno. 2012. "Traffic Engineering: Road Diets." Fresno, CA. http://www.fresno.gov/Government/DepartmentDirectory /PublicWorks/TrafficEngineering/RoadDiets.htm.

City of Moscow. 2010. *City of Moscow Large Retail Establishments Design Manual*. Moscow, ID: City of Moscow. http://www.moscow .id.us/comm_dev/documents/LRE_Design_manual.pdf.

City of Ottawa. 2007. *Transit-Oriented Development Guidelines*. Ottawa, ON: City of Ottawa.

City of Portland. 2009. "Development Standards in Commercial Zones" (Zoning Code Section 33.130. 215). *Zoning Code Information Guide*. Portland, OR: City of Portland. http://www.portlandonline.com/BDS /index.cfm?a=92200.

City of Seattle. 2005. *Capitol Hill Neighborhood Design Guidelines*. Seattle: City of Seattle. http://www.seattle.gov/dpd/cms/groups /pan/@pan/@plan/@designguideupdate/documents /web_informational/dpds018800.pdf.

———. 2007. *North District/Lake City Neighborhoods Design Guidelines*. Seattle: City of Seattle. http://www.seattle.gov/dpd /cms/groups/pan/@pan/@plan/@drp/documents/web_informational /dpdp_019504.pdf.

CNU (Congress of New Urbanism). 2003. *New Urban Projects on a Neighborhood Scale in the United States*. Ithaca, NY: New Urban News.

Cortright, J. 2008. "Driven to the Brink: How the Gas Price Spike Popped the Housing Bubble and Devalued the Suburbs." White paper, CEOs for Cities. http://community-wealth.com/_pdfs/articles-publications/tod/paper-cortwright.pdf.

Crankshaw, N. 2009. *Creating Vibrant Public Spaces: Streetscape Design in Commercial and Historic Districts*. Washington, DC: Island Press.

Cullen, G. 1961. *The Concise Townscape*. London: Reed Educational and Professional Publishing.

Dehring, C., and N. Dunse. 2006. "Housing Density and the Effect of Proximity to Public Open Space in Aberdeen, Scotland." *Real Estate Economics* 34 (4): 553–66.

Denis, J., and D. Pontille. 2010. "Placing Subway Signs: Practical Properties of Signs at Work." *Visual Communication* 9 (4): 441–62.

Diez Roux, A.V., and C. Mair. 2010. "Neighborhoods and Health." *Annals of the New York Academy of Sciences* 1186: 125–45.

DiLaura, D.L. 2011. *The Lighting Handbook: Reference and Application*. New York: Illuminating Engineering Society of North America.

Dittmar, H., and G. Ohland. 2004. *The New Transit Town: Best Practices in Transit-Oriented Development*. Washington, DC: Island Press.

Donovan, G.H., and D.T. Butry. 2010. "Trees in the City: Valuing Street Trees in Portland, Oregon." *Landscape and Urban Planning* 94 (2): 77–83.

Dougald, L.E. 2004. *Development of Guidelines for the Installation of Marked Crosswalks*. Charlottesville: Virginia Transportation Research Council.

Duany, A., and E. Plater-Zyberk. 1992. "The Second Coming of the American Small Town." *Wilson Quarterly* 16 (Winter): 19–48.

Dumbaugh, E. 2006a. "The Design of Safe Urban Roadsides." *Transportation Research Record* 1971: 74–82.

———. 2006b. "Enhancing the Safety and Operational Performance of Arterial Roadways in the Atlanta Metropolitan Region." Report submitted to the Atlanta Regional Commission.

Dumbaugh, E., and W. Li. 2011. "Designing for the Safety of Pedestrians, Cyclists, and Motorists in Urban Environments." *Journal of the American Planning Association* 77 (1): 69–88.

Dumbaugh, E., and R. Rae. 2009. "Safe Urban Form: Revisiting the Relationship between Community Design and Traffic Safety." *Journal of the American Planning Association* 75 (3): 309–29.

Duncan, M.J., J.C. Spence, and W.K. Mummery. 2005. "Perceived Environment and Physical Activity: A Meta-Analysis of Selected Environmental Characteristics." *International Journal of Behavioral Nutrition and Physical Activity* 2: 11.

Dunphy, R.T., R. Cervero, F.C. Dock, M. McAvery, D.R. Porter, and C.J. Swenson. 2004. *Developing around Transit: Strategies and Solutions That Work*. Washington, DC: Urban Land Institute.

Ehrenfeucht, R., and A. Loukaitou-Sideris. 2010. "Planning Urban Sidewalks: Infrastructure, Daily Life and Destinations." *Journal of Urban Design* 15 (4): 459–71.

Ellin, N. 2010. "Canalscape: Practising Integral Urbanism in Metropolitan Phoenix." *Journal of Urban Design* 15 (4): 599–610.

Elshestaway, Y. 1997. "Urban Complexity: Toward the Measurement of the Physical Complexity of Streetscapes." *Journal of Architectural and Planning Research* 2 (4): 301–16.

Elvik, R. 1995. "Meta-Analysis of Evaluations of Public Lighting as Accident Countermeasure." *Transportation Research Record* 1485: 112–23.

———. 2001. "Area-Wide Urban Traffic Calming Schemes: A Meta-Analysis of Safety Effects." *Accident Analysis & Prevention* 33 (3): 327–36.

Engwicht, D. 1993. *Reclaiming Our Cities and Towns: Better Living with Less Traffic*. Philadelphia: New Society Publishers.

Eppli, M.J., and C.C. Tu. 1999. *Valuing the New Urbanism: The Impact of the New Urbanism on Prices of Single-Family Homes*. Washington, DC: Urban Land Institute.

———. 2007. "Market Acceptance of Single-Family Housing in Smart Growth Communities." http://www.epa.gov/smartgrowth /pdf/eppli_tu.pdf.

Evans, J.E., R.H. Pratt, R. Stryker, and J.R. Kuzmyak. 2007. "Transit Oriented Development." Chap. 17 in *TCRP Report 95: Traveler Response to Transportation System Changes*. Washington, DC: Transportation Research Board.

Ewald, W.R. 1977. *Street Graphics: A Concept and a System*. McLean, VA: Landscape Architecture Foundation.

Ewan, R.F. 2002. "Creating a 'There' There." *Landscape Architecture* 92 (4): 84–91.

Ewing, R. 1977. *Transportation and Land Use Innovations*. Chicago: American Planning Association.

———. 1992. "Roadway Levels of Service in an Era of Growth Management." *Transportation Research Record* 1364: 63–70.

———. 1993. "Transportation Service Standards: As If People Matter." *Transportation Research Record* 1400: 10–17.

———. 1996. *Best Development Practices: Doing the Right Thing and Making Money at the Same Time*. Chicago: American Planning Association.

———. 1997. "Is Los Angeles-Style Sprawl Desirable?" *Journal of the American Planning Association* 63 (1): 107–26.

———. 1999. *Traffic Calming: State-of-the-Practice*. Washington, DC: Institute of Transportation Engineers.

———. 2000a. "Asking Transit Users about Transit-Oriented Design." *Transportation Research Record* 1735: 19–24.

———. 2000b. "Sketch Planning a Street Network." *Transportation Research Record* 1722: 75–79.

Ewing, R., and S. Brown. 2009a. "Traffic Calming Progress Report." *Planning* 75 (10): 32–35.

———. 2009b. *U.S. Traffic Calming Manual*. Chicago: American Planning Association/American Society of Civil Engineers.

Ewing, R., O. Clemente, S. Handy, R. Brownson, and E. Winston. 2005. *Identifying and Measuring Urban Design Qualities Related to Walkability: Final Report*. Princeton, NJ: Robert Wood Johnson Foundation. http://www.activelivingresearch.org/files/FinalReport_071605.pdf.

Ewing, R., and E. Dumbaugh. 2009. "The Built Environment and Traffic Safety: A Review of Empirical Evidence." *Journal of Planning Literature* 23 (4): 347–67.

Ewing, R., M. Greenwald, M. Zhang, J. Walters, M. Feldman, R. Cervero, L.D. Frank, and J. Thomas. 2011. "Traffic Generated by Mixed-Use Developments: A Six-Region Study Using Consistent Built Environmental Measures," *Journal of Urban Planning and Development* 137 (3): 248–62.

Ewing R., and S. Handy. 2009. "Measuring the Unmeasurable: Urban Design Qualities Related to Walkability." *Journal of Urban Design* 14 (1): 65–84.

Ewing, R., S. Handy, R. Brownson, O. Clemente, and E. Winston. 2006. "Identifying and Measuring Urban Design Qualities Related to Walkability." *Journal of Physical Activity and Health* 3 (Suppl 1): S223–40.

Ewing, R., and M. King. 2002. *Flexible Design of New Jersey's Main Streets*. Ewing: New Jersey Department of Transportation.

Ewing, R., T. Stevens, and S. Brown. 2007. "Skinny Streets and Fire Trucks." *Urban Land* 66 (8): 121–23.

Fan, Y., and A.J. Khattak. 2008. "Urban Form, Individual Spatial Footprints, and Travel Examination of Space-Use Behavior." *Transportation Research Record* 2082: 98–106.

Farrington, D.P., and B.C. Welsh. 2002. "Effects of Improved Street Lighting on Crime: A Systematic Review." Home Office Research Study no. 251, Home Office Research, Development and Statistics Directorate, London.

FDOT (Florida Department of Transportation). 2002. *Quality/Level of Service Handbook*. Tallahassee: FDOT.

Fendley, T. 2009. "Making Sense of the City: A Collection of Design Principles for Urban Wayfinding." *Information Design Journal* 17 (2): 91–108.

FHWA (Federal Highway Administration). 2001. *Geometric Design Practices for European Roads*. Report no. FHWA-PL-01-026. Washington, DC: U.S. Department of Transportation.

———. 2003. *Manual on Uniform Traffic Control Devices for Streets and Highways*. 2003 ed. Washington, DC: U.S. Government Printing Office.

Fischer, E.L., G.K. Rousseau, S.M. Turner, E.J. Blais, C.L. Engelhart, D.R. Henderson, J.A. Kaplan, et al. 2010. *Pedestrian and Bicyclist Safety and Mobility in Europe*. Washington, DC: Federal Highway Administration.

Fitzpatrick, K., K.M. Hall, S. Farnsworth, and M.D. Finley. 2001. "Evaluation of Bus Bulbs." TCRP Report no. 65. Transportation Research Board, Washington, DC.

Fitzpatrick, K., S. Turner, M. Brewer, P. Carlson, B. Ullman, N. Trout, E.S. Park, J. Whitacre, N. Lalani, and D. Lord. 2006. *Improving Pedestrian Safety at Unsignalized Crossing*. TCRP Report no. 112/NCHRP Report no. 562. Washington, DC: Transportation Research Board.

Fitzpatrick, K., B. Ullman, and N. Trout. 2004. "On-Street Pedestrian Surveys of Pedestrian Crossing Treatments." *TRB 83rd Annual Meeting Compendium of Papers*. Washington, DC: Transportation Research Board. CD-ROM.

Fleming, R.L. 2002. *Saving Face: How Corporate Franchise Design Can Respect Community Identity*. Rev. ed. Chicago: American Planning Association.

———. 2007. *The Art of Placemaking: Interpreting Community through Public Art and Urban Design*. New York: Merrill Publishing.

Fleming, R.L., and R. von Tscharner. 1981. *Place Makers: Public Art That Tells You Where You Are*. Cambridge, MA: Townscape Institute.

Forsyth, A., J. Jacobson, and K. Thering. 2010. "Six Assessments of the Same Places: Comparing Views of Urban Design." *Journal of Urban Design* 15 (1): 21–48.

FPSC (Florida Public Service Commission). 2007. *July 2007 Report to the Legislature on Enhancing the Reliability of Florida's Distribution and Transmission Grids during Extreme Weather*. Tallahassee: FPSC. http://www.floridapsc.com/publications/pdf/electricgas/stormhardening2007.pdf.

Fruin, J.J. 1971. *Pedestrian Planning and Design*. New York: Metropolitan Association of Urban Designers and Environmental Planners Inc.

FTA (Federal Transit Administration). 1996. *Art in Transit … Making It Happen*. Washington, DC: FTA. http://www.fta.dot.gov/printer_friendly/about_FTA_3529.html.

Gaffkin, F., M. McEldowney, and K. Sterrett. 2010. "Creating Shared Public Space in the Contested City: The Role of Urban Design." *Journal of Urban Design* 15 (4): 493–513.

Garten, C. 2009. "A Watershed Moment for Public Art in Calgary." *Public Art Review* 20 (2): 82–83.

Garvin, A. 2000. "An Insider's View." *Planning* 66 (3): 4–10.

Gehl, J. 1987. *Life between Buildings: Using Public Space*. New York: Van Nostrand Reinhold.

———. 2010. *Cities for People*. Washington, DC: Island Press.

Gehl, J., L.J. Kaefer, and S. Reigstad. 2006. "Close Encounters with Buildings." *Urban Design International* 11: 29–47.

Geisler, W.S., and D.G. Albrecht. 2000. "Spatial Vision." In *Seeing*, ed. K.K. DeValois, pp. 79–128. San Diego, CA: Academic Press.

Gibbons, J., and B. Oberholzer. 1992. *Urban Streetscapes: A Workbook for Designers*. New York: Van Nostrand Reinhold.

Girling, C., and R. Kellett. 2005. *Skinny Streets & Green Neighborhoods: Design for Environment and Community*. Washington, DC: Island Press.

Glatting Jackson Kercher Anglin Lopez Rinehart Inc. 1994. *Central Florida Mobility Design Manual*. Orlando: Central Florida Regional Transportation Authority.

Handy, S. 2005. "Critical Assessment of the Literature on the Relationships among Transportation, Land Use, and Physical Activity." Resource paper for TRB Special Report 282, *Does the Built Environment Influence Physical Activity? Examining the Evidence*. Washington, DC: Transportation Research Board and Institute of Medicine.

Handy, S., R.G. Paterson, and K. Butler. 2003. *Planning for Street Connectivity: Getting from Here to There*. Chicago: American Planning Association.

Handy, S., J.F. Sallis, D. Weber, E. Maibach, and M. Hollander. 2008. "Is Support for Traditionally Designed Communities Growing? Evidence from Two National Surveys." *Journal of the American Planning Association* 74 (2): 209–21.

Harkey, D.L., and C.V. Zegeer. 2004. *PEDSAFE: Pedestrian Safety Guide and Countermeasure Selection System*. Report no. FHWA-SA-04-003. Washington, DC: Federal Highway Administration.

Hartnett, J. 2008. "*Si Quis Hic Sederit*: Streetside Benches and Urban Society in Pompeii." *American Journal of Archaeology* 112 (1): 91–119.

Hayden, D., and J. Wark. 2004. *A Field Guide to Sprawl*. New York: Norton.

Haywood, R. 2008. "Underneath the Arches in the East End: An Evaluation of the Planning and Design Policy Context of the East London Line Extension Project." *Journal of Urban Design* 13 (3): 361–85.

Hazelrigg, G. 2006. "A Gem of a Park in Portland's Cultured Pearl." *Landscape Architecture* 96 (3): 26–33.

Heath, G.W., R.C. Brownson, J. Kruger, R. Miles, K.E. Powell, L.T. Ramsey, and the Task Force on Community Preventive Services. 2006. "The Effectiveness of Urban Design and Land Use and Transport Policies and Practices to Increase Physical Activity: A Systematic Review." *Journal of Physical Activity and Health* 3 (1): 55–76.

Heath, T., S. Smith, and B. Lim. 2000. "The Complexity of Tall Building Facades." *Journal of Architectural and Planning Research* 17 (3): 206–20.

Hedman, R. 1984. *Fundamentals of Urban Design*. Chicago: American Planning Association.

Herzog, T.R., S. Kaplan, and R. Kaplan. 1982. "The Prediction of Preference for Unfamiliar Urban Places." *Population and Environment* 5: 43–59.

Higashiyama, A. 2008. "Map Information Helping Us to Find a Way to the Goal." *Bulletin of the Japanese Cognitive Science Society* 15 (1): 51–61.

Hoppenbrouwer, E., and E. Louw. 2005. "Mixed-Use Development: Theory and Practice in Amsterdam's Eastern Docklands." *European Planning Studies* 13 (7): 967–83.

Huang, H.F., J.R. Stewart, and C.V. Zegeer. 2002. "Evaluation of Lane Reduction 'Road Diet' Measures on Crashes and Injuries." *Transportation Research Record* 1784: 80–90.

IDA and IESNA (International Dark-Sky Association and Illuminating Engineering Society of North America). 2011. *Model Lighting Ordinance (MLO) with User's Guide*. http://www.ies.org/PDF/MLO /MLO_FINAL_June2011.pdf.

ITE (Institute of Transportation Engineers). 2008. *Trip Generation*. 8th ed. Washington, DC: Institute of Transportation Engineers.

ITE Technical Council Committee 5A-25A. 1984. *Recommended Guidelines for Subdivision Streets*. Washington, DC: Institute of Transportation Engineers.

Ivan, J.N., N.W. Garrick, and G. Hansen. 2009. "Designing Roads That Guide Drivers to Choose Safer Speeds." Connecticut Department of Transportation, Rocky Hill.

Jacobs, A. 1993. *Great Streets*. Cambridge, MA: MIT Press.

Jacobs, A., and D. Appleyard. 1987. "Toward an Urban Design Manifesto." *Journal of the American Planning Association* 53 (1): 112–20.

Jacobs, A., E. Macdonald, and Y. Rofe. 2002. *The Boulevard Book: History, Evolution, Design of Multiway Boulevards*. Cambridge, MA: MIT Press.

Jacobs, J. 1961. *The Death and Life of Great American Cities*. New York: Random House.

Jago, R., T. Baranowski, I. Zakeri, and M. Harris. 2005. "Observed Environmental Features and the Physical Activity of Adolescent Males." *American Journal of Preventative Medicine* 29 (2): 98–104.

Jost, D. 2007. "Betting on a More Walkable Future." *Landscape Architecture* 97 (5): 122–31.

Kaczynski, A.T. 2010. "Neighborhood Walkability Perceptions: Associations with Amount of Neighborhood-Based Physical Activity by Intensity and Purpose." *Journal of Physical Activity and Health* 7 (1): 3–10.

Kaplan, R., and S. Kaplan. 1989. *The Experience of Nature: A Psychological Perspective*. New York: Cambridge University Press.

Kay, J.H. 1997. *Asphalt Nation: How the Automobile Took Over America, and How We Can Take It Back*. Berkeley: University of California Press.

Kayden, J.S. 2000. *Privately Owned Public Space: The New York City Experience*. New York: John Wiley & Sons.

Kenyon, J.B. 1987. "A Model of Downtown Pedestrian Generation." In *Getting There by All Means: Interrelationships of Transportation Modes*, pp. 233–37. Boulder, CO: 8th International Pedestrian Conference.

Kiefer, M.J. 2001. "Privatizing Creation of the Public Realm: The Fruits of New York City's Incentive Zoning Ordinance." *Boston College Environmental Affairs Law Review* 28 (4): 637–50.

Kim, J, G.F. Ulfarsson, V.N. Shankar, and F.L. Mannering. 2010. "A Note on Modeling Pedestrian-Injury Severity in Motor-Vehicle Crashes with the Mixed Logit Model." *Accident Analysis & Prevention* 42 (6): 1751–58.

King, M.R. 1999. "Calming New York City Intersections." Paper presented at the Urban Street Symposium, Dallas, TX, June 28–30.

Kittelson & Associates. 2003. *Transit Capacity and Quality of Service Manual*. 2nd ed. Washington, DC: Transportation Research Board.

Knoblauch, R.L., M. Nitzburg, and R.F. Seifert. 2001. *Pedestrian Crosswalk Case Studies: Sacramento, California; Richmond, Virginia; Buffalo, New York; Stillwater, Minnesota*. Report no. FHWA-RD-00-103. Washington, DC: Federal Highway Administration.

Knoblauch, R.L., B.H. Tustin, S.A. Smith, and M.T. Pietrucha. 1988. *Investigation of Exposure-Based Pedestrian Accident Areas: Crosswalks, Sidewalks, Local Streets and Major Arterials*. Report no. FHWA-RD-87-038. Washington, DC: Federal Highway Administration.

Knudsen, B., R. Florida, K. Stolarick, and G. Gates. 2009. "Density and Creativity in U.S. Regions." *Annals of the Association of American Geographers* 98 (2): 461–78.

Krahnstover-Davison, K., and C.T. Lawson. 2006. "Do Attributes in the Physical Environment Influence Children's Physical Activity? A Review of the Literature." *International Journal of Behavioral Nutrition and Physical Activity* 3 (19).

Kroloff, R. 1996. "From Infrastructure to Identity." *Places* 10 (3): 56–57.

Kunstler, J.H. 1993. *The Geography of Nowhere: The Rise and Decline of America's Man-Made Landscape*. New York: Simon & Schuster.

Lachman, M. Leanne, and Deborah L. Brett. *Generation Y: America's New Housing Wave*. Washington, D.C.: Urban Land Institute, 2011.

Lacy, K., R. Srinivasan, C.V. Zegeer, R. Pfefer, T.R. Neuman, K.L. Slack, and K.K. Hardy. 2004. *Volume 08: A Guide for Reducing Collisions Involving Utility Poles*. Washington, DC: Transportation Research Board.

Landis, B.W., V.R. Vattikitti, R.M. Ottenberg, D.S. McLeod, and M. Guttenplan. 2001. "Modeling the Roadside Walking Environment: Pedestrian LOS." *Transportation Research Record* 1773: 82–88.

Lansing, J. 2003. *Portland: People, Politics, and Power, 1851–2001*. Corvallis: Oregon State University Press.

Larsen, K., J. Gilliland, P. Hess, P. Tucker, J. Irwin, and M. He. 2009. "The Influence of the Physical Environment and Sociodemographic Characteristics on Children's Mode of Travel to and from School." *American Journal of Public Health* 99 (3): 520–26.

Laurence, P.L. 2006. "The Death and Life of Urban Design: Jane Jacobs, the Rockefeller Foundation and the New Research in Urbanism, 1955–1965." *Journal of Urban Design* 11 (2): 145–72.

Leinberger, C. 2008. *The Option of Urbanism: Investing in a New American Dream*. Washington, DC: Island Press.

Lennard, S.H.C. 2008. *Genius of the European Square: How Europe's Traditional Multi-Functional Squares Support Social Life and Civic Engagement*. Carmel, CA: Gondolier Press.

Lennard, S.H.C., and H.L. Lennard. 1987. *Livable Cities—People and Places: Social and Design Principles for the Future of the City*. South Hampton, NY: Center for Urban Well-Being.

Levine, J., and L. Frank. 2007. "Transportation and Land-Use Preferences and Residents' Neighborhood Choices: The Sufficiency of Compact Development in the Atlanta Region." *Transportation* 34 (2): 255–74.

Levine, J., A. Inam, and G.W. Torng. 2005. "A Choice-Based Rationale for Land Use and Transportation Alternatives: Evidence from Boston and Atlanta." *Journal of Planning Education and Research* 24 (3): 317–30.

Lewis, P.G., and M. Baldassare. 2010. "The Complexity of Public Attitudes toward Compact Development: Survey Evidence from Five States." *Journal of the American Planning Association* 76 (2): 219–37.

Liggett, R., A. Loukaitou-Sideris, and H. Iseki. 2001. "The Bus Stop–Environment Connection: Do Characteristics of the Built Environment Correlate with Bus Stop Crime?" *Transportation Research Record* 1760: 20–27.

Lin, D., and H. Luo. 2004. "Fading and Color Changes in Colored Asphalt Quantified by the Image Analysis Method." *Construction and Building Materials* 18 (4): 255–61.

Litman, T. 2011. "Roadway Connectivity: Creating More Connected Roadway and Pathway Networks." In *Transportation Demand Management Encyclopedia*. Victoria, BC: Victoria Transport Policy Institute. http://www.vtpi.org/tdm/tdm116.htm.

Llewelyn-Davies. 2000. *Urban Design Compendium*. London: English Partnerships/Housing Corporation.

Lohan Associates. 1996. *Guidelines for Transit-Supportive Development*. Chicago: Chicago Transit Authority.

Loukaitou-Sideris, A., and T. Banerjee. 1998. *Urban Design Downtown: Poetics and Politics of Form*. Berkeley: University of California Press.

Loukaitou-Sideris, A., R. Liggett, H. Iseki, and W. Thurlow. 2001. "Measuring the Effects of Built Environment on Bus Stop Crime." *Environment and Planning B: Planning and Design* 28 (2): 255–80.

Lucy, W.H., and D.L. Phillips. 2006. *Tomorrow's Cities, Tomorrow's Suburbs*. Chicago: Planners Press.

Lynch, K. 1960. *The Image of the City*. Cambridge, MA: Joint Center for Urban Studies.

———. 1971. *Site Planning*. 2nd ed. Cambridge, MA: MIT Press.

Lynch, K., and G. Hack. 1984. *Site Planning*. 3rd ed. Cambridge, MA: MIT Press.

Macdonald, E. 2005. "Street-Facing Dwelling Units and Livability: The Impacts of Emerging Building Types in Vancouver's New High-Density Residential Neighborhoods." *Journal of Urban Design* 10 (1): 13–38.

———. 2006. "Building a Boulevard." *Access* 28: 2–11.

Mandelker, D. 2004. *Street Graphics and the Law*. Chicago, IL: APA Planners Press.

Marshall, W.E., and N.W. Garrick. 2010. "Effect of Street Network Design on Walking and Biking." *Transportation Research Record* 2198: 103–15.

Marshall, W.E., N.W. Garrick, and G. Hansen. 2008. "Reassessing On-Street Parking." *Transportation Research Record* 2046: 45–52.

Martin, J. 2008. "Cities Rack Up Public Artwork with Bike Racks." *USA Today*, November 3.

Mathew Greenwald & Associates. 2003. *These Four Walls ... Americans 45+ Talk about Home and Community*. Washington, DC: AARP.

McCarthy, J. 2006. "Regeneration of Cultural Quarters: Public Art for Place Image or Place Identity?" *Journal of Urban Design* 11 (2): 243–62.

McCormack, G.R., M. Rock, A.M. Toohey, and D. Hignell. 2010. "Characteristics of Urban Parks Associated with Park Use and Physical Activity: A Review of Qualitative Research." *Health & Place* 16 (4): 712–26.

McDonald, S.S. 2007. *The Parking Garage: Design and Evolution of a Modern Urban Form*. Washington, DC: Urban Land Institute.

McKone, J. 2010. "Next Stop? Crowdsourced Bus Shelters." *TheCityFix* (blog), October 7. http://thecityfix.com/blog/crowdsourcing-bus-stop-designs/.

McMillan, T.E. 2005. "Urban Form and a Child's Trip to School: The Current Literature and a Framework for Future Research." *Journal of Planning Literature* 19 (4): 440–56.

Mehta, V. 2009. "Look Closely and You Will See, Listen Carefully and You Will Hear: Urban Design and Social Interaction on Streets." *Journal of Urban Design* 14 (1): 29–64.

Merom, D., A. Bauman, P. Phongsavan, E. Cerin, M. Kassis, W. Brown, B.J. Smith, and C. Rissel. 2009. "Can a Motivational Intervention Overcome an Unsupportive Environment for Walking: Findings from the Step-by-Step Study." *Annals of Behavioral Medicine* 38 (2): 137–46.

Messenger, T., and R. Ewing. 1996. "Transit-Oriented Development in the Sunbelt." *Transportation Research Record* 1552: 145–52.

Metz, D., and C. Below. 2011. *Key Findings from Recent Southern California Survey on Transportation and Land Use Planning*. Santa Monica: Fairbank, Maslin, Maullin, Metz & Associates.

Millward, A.A., and S. Sabir. 2011. "Benefits of a Forested Urban Park: What Is the Value of Allan Gardens to the City of Toronto, Canada?" *Landscape and Urban Planning* 100 (3): 177–88.

Montgomery, J. 1997. "Café Culture and the City: The Role of Pavement Cafés." *Journal of Urban Design* 2 (1): 83–103.

Morrow-Jones, H., E. Irwin, and B. Rowe. 2004. "Consumer Preference for Neotraditional Neighborhood Characteristics." *Housing Policy Debate* 15 (1): 171–202.

Moudon, A.V., C. Lee, A.D. Cheadle, C. Garvin, D.B. Johnson, T.L. Schmid, and R.D. Weathers. 2007. "Attributes of Environments Supporting Walking." *American Journal of Health Promotion* 21 (5): 448–59.

Murray, A., and X. Wu. 2003. "Accessibility Tradeoffs in Public Transit Planning." *Journal of Geographical Systems* 5 (1): 93–107.

Naderi, J.R., B.S. Kweon, and P. Maghelal. 2008. "The Street Tree Effect and Driver Safety." *ITE Journal* 78 (2): 69–73.

Nasar, J.L. 1987. "The Effect of Sign Complexity and Coherence on the Perceived Quality of Retail Scenes." *Journal of the American Planning Association* 53 (4): 499–509.

Nasar, J.L., and Y. Lin. 2003. "Evaluative Responses to Five Kinds of Water Features." *Landscape Research* 28 (4): 441–50.

Nelessen, A.C. 1994. *Visions for a New American Dream: Process, Principles, and an Ordinance to Plan and Design Small Communities*. Chicago, IL: APA Planners Press.

Nelson, A.C. 2006. "Leadership in a New Era." *Journal of the American Planning Association* 72 (4): 393–407.

Newman, P., and T. Hogan. 1981 "A Review of Urban Density Models: Toward a Resolution of the Conflict between Populace and Planner." *Human Ecology* 9 (3): 269–303.

Nordh, H., C. Alalouch, and T. Hartig. 2011. "Assessing Restorative Components of Small Urban Parks Using Conjoint Methodology." *Urban Forestry & Urban Greening* 10 (2): 95–103.

Oldenburg, R. 1991. *The Great Good Place*. New York: Paragon House.

Paumier, C. 2004. *Creating a Vibrant City Center*. Washington, DC: Urban Land Institute.

PBIC and APBP (Pedestrian and Bicycle Information Center and Association of Pedestrian and Bicycle Professionals). 2009. "Case Study Compendium." University of North Carolina Highway Safety Research Center, Chapel Hill. http://www.walkinginfo.org/case_studies.

Peters, K., B. Elands, and A. Buijs. 2010. "Social Interactions in Urban Parks: Stimulating Social Cohesion?" *Urban Forestry & Urban Greening* 9 (2): 93–100.

Plaut, P.O., and M.G. Boarnet. 2003. "New Urbanism and the Value of Neighborhood Design." *Journal of Architectural and Planning Research* 20 (3): 254–65.

Pratt, R.H., and J.E. Evans. 2004. "Bus Routing and Coverage." Chap. 10 in *TCRP Report 95:Traveler Response to Transportation System Changes*. Washington, DC: Transportation Research Board.

Pratt, R.H., K.F. Turnbull, I.V. Evans, E. John, B.E. McCollom, F. Spielberg, et al. 1999. *Traveler Response to Transportation System Changes: Interim Handbook*. Washington, DC: Transportation Research Board.

Price, G. 2000. "Another Crack at the Suburbs." *Journal of the American Planning Association* 66 (4): 360–63.

Proft, J., and P. Condon. 2001. *Transportation and Community Design: The Effects of Land Use, Density, and Street Pattern on Travel Behavior*. Vancouver: University of British Columbia.

Project for Public Spaces. 2001. *How to Turn a Place Around: A Handbook for Creating Successful Public Spaces*. New York: Project for Public Spaces.

———. 2009. "Bus Shelters." In *Public Space Amenities: A Guide to Their Design and Management in Downtowns, Neighborhood Commercial Districts, and Parks*. http://www.pps.org/reference /busshelters/.

Project for Public Spaces/Multisystems. 1999. *The Role of Transit Amenities and Vehicle Characteristics in Building Transit Ridership: Amenities for Transit Handbook and the Transit Design Game Workbook*. Washington DC: National Academy Press.

Pushkarev, B.S., and J.M. Zupan. 1975. *Urban Space for Pedestrians*. Cambridge, MA: MIT Press.

———. 1977. *Public Transportation and Land Use Policy*. Bloomington: Indiana University Press.

Rapoport, A. 1990. *History and Precedent in Environmental Design*. New York: Plenum Press, Kluwer Academic Publishers.

Ray, B. 2008. *Guidelines for Selection of Speed Reduction Techniques at High-Speed Intersections*. NCHRP Report no. 613. Washington, DC: Transportation Research Board.

Rea, M.S., J.D. Bullough, C.R. Fay, J.A. Brons, J. Van Derlofske, and E.T. Donnell. 2009. *Review of the Safety Benefits and Other Effects of Roadway Lighting*. Washington, DC: Transportation Research Board.

Ream, J., and S. Martin. 2007. *Denver Strategic Parking Plan: Phase 1 Report*. Denver, CO: City and County of Denver.

Residential Streets Task Force. 1990. *Residential Streets*. Washington, DC: American Society of Civil Engineers/National Association of Home Builders/Urban Land Institute.

Reynolds, K.D., J. Wolch, J. Byrne, C. Chou, G. Feng, S. Weaver, and M. Jerrett. 2007. "Trail Characteristics as Correlates of Urban Trail Use." *American Journal of Health Promotion* 21 (4 Suppl): 335–47.

Rifaat, S.M., R. Tay, and A. de Barros. 2011. "Effect of Street Pattern on the Severity of Crashes Involving Vulnerable Road Users." *Accident Analysis & Prevention* 43 (1): 276–83.

Robaton, A. 2005. "Lifestyle Centers Compete for Retailers." *Shopping Centers Today*, February. http://www.icsc.org/srch/sct/sct0205 /cover_3.php.

Robertson, K.A. 1993. "Pedestrianization Strategies for Downtown Planners." *Journal of the American Planning Association* 59 (3): 361–71.

Rodgers, K., and K. Roy. 2010. *Cartopia: Portland's Food Cart Revolution*. Portland, OR: Roy Rodgers Press.

Roman, C.G., and A. Chalfin. 2008. "Fear of Walking Outdoors: A Multilevel Ecologic Analysis of Crime and Disorder." *American Journal of Preventive Medicine* 34 (4): 306–12.

Ronit, E. 2009. "Public Art Master Planning: Developing a Plan for Your Community." *Public Art Review* 20 (2): 88–89.

Rosales, J. 2006. *Road Diet Handbook: Setting Trends for Livable Streets*. New York: Parsons Brinckerhoff.

Rowley, A. 1996. "Mixed-Use Development: Ambiguous Concept, Simplistic Analysis and Wishful Thinking?" *Planning Practice and Research* 11 (4): 85–97.

Russ, T.H. 2002. *Site Planning and Design Handbook*. New York: McGraw-Hill.

Ryan, B. 2008. "The Restructuring of Detroit: City Block Form Change in a Shrinking City, 1900–2000." *Urban Design International* 13 (3): 156–68.

Ryan, M. 2000. "The Road to Chaos." *Architect's Journal* 212 (12): 40.

Salingaros, N.A. 2000. "Complexity and Urban Coherence." *Journal of Urban Design* 5 (3): 291–317.

Sandt, L. 2011. *Residents Guide for Creating Safe and Walkable Communities*. Washington, DC: U.S. Department of Transportation.

Schmitz, A. 2006. *Creating Walkable Places: Compact Mixed-Use Solutions*. Washington, DC: Urban Land Institute.

Schwanke, D., C. Lockwood, P.L. Phillips, S. Fader, F. Spink, D. Versel, L. Holst, et al. 2003. *Mixed-Use Development Handbook*. 2nd ed. Washington, DC: Urban Land Institute.

Shaftoe, H. 2008. *Convivial Urban Spaces: Creating Effective Public Places*. Oxford, UK: Earthscan/Taylor and Francis Group.

Shoup, D.C. 2005. *The High Cost of Free Parking*. Chicago: Planners Press.

Siksna, A. 1997. "The Effects of Block Size and Form in North American and Australian City Centres." *Urban Morphology* 1 (1): 19–33.

———. 1998. "City Centre Blocks and Their Evolution: A Comparative Study of Eight American and Australian CBDs." *Journal of Urban Design* 3 (3): 253–84.

Skjaeveland, O. 2001. "Effects of Street Parks on Social Interactions among Neighbors: A Place Perspective." *Journal of Architectural and Planning Research* 18 (2): 131–47.

Smith, M. 2005. *Shared Parking*. 2nd ed. Washington, DC: Urban Land Institute, and International Council of Shopping Centers.

Smith, S.A., K.S. Opiela, L.L. Impett, M.T. Pietrucha, R. Knoblauch, and C. Kubat. 1987. *Planning and Implementing Pedestrian Facilities in Suburban and Developing Rural Areas*. National Cooperative Highway Research Program Report no. 294A. Washington, DC: Transportation Research Board.

Soares, A.L., F.C. Rego, E.G. McPherson, J.R. Simpson, P.J. Peper, and Q. Xiao. 2011. "Benefits and Costs of Street Trees in Lisbon, Portugal." *Urban Forestry & Urban Greening* 10 (2): 69–78.

Song, Y., and G.J. Knaap. 2003. "New Urbanism and Housing Values: A Disaggregate Assessment." *Journal of Urban Economics* 54 (2): 218–38.

Southworth, S., and P.M. Owens. 1993. "The Evolving Metropolis: Studies of Community, Neighborhood, and Street Form at the Urban Edge." *Journal of the American Planning Association* 59 (3): 271–87.

Stamps, A.E. 1998. "Measures of Architectural Mass: From Vague Impressions to Definite Design Features." *Environment and Planning B* 25: 825–36.

———. 1999. "Physical Determinants of Preferences for Residential Facades." *Environment and Behavior* 31 (6): 723–51.

Steuteville, R. 2009. "The Case for the Simple Grid." *New Urban News* 14 (2): 1, 4–5.

Stout, T.B., M. Pawlovich, R.R. Souleyrette, and A. Carriquiry. 2006. "Safety Impacts of 'Road Diets' in Iowa." Iowa Department of Transportation. http://www.iowadot.gov/crashanalysis/pdfs /ite_draft_4to3laneconversion_papersubmission_2005.pdf.

StreetsWiki. 2012. "Woonerf." http://streetswiki.wikispaces.com /woonerf.

Stubbs, M. 2002. "Car Parking and Residential Development: Sustainability, Design and Planning Policy, and Perceptions of Parking Provision." *Journal of Urban Design* 7 (2): 213–37.

Stucki, P. 2003. "Obstacles in Pedestrian Simulations." Master's thesis, Swiss Institute of Technology ETH, Zurich.

Sucher, D. 1995. *City Comforts: How to Build an Urban Village*. Seattle: City Comforts Press.

Talen, E. 2000. "Measuring the Public Realm: A Preliminary Assessment of the Link between Public Space and Sense of Community." *Journal of Architectural and Planning Research* 17 (4): 344–60.

———. 2010. "The Spatial Logic of Parks." *Journal of Urban Design* 15 (4): 473–91.

Texas Transportation Institute. 1996. *Report 19: Guidelines for the Location and Design of Bus Stops*. Washington, DC: National Academy Press.

Thibaud, J. 2001. "Frames of Visibility in Public Spaces." *Places* 14 (1): 12–17.

Tolley, R. 1990. *Calming Traffic in Residential Areas*. Brefi, UK: Brefi Press.

Trancik, R. 1986. *Finding Lost Space: Theories of Urban Design*. New York: Van Nostrand Reinhold.

TRB (Transportation Research Board). 2000. *Highway Capacity Manual*. Washington, DC: National Research Council.

Tunnard, C., and B. Pushkarev. 1963. *Man-Made America: Chaos or Control?* New Haven, CT: Yale University Press.

ULI and PWC (Urban Land Institute and PricewaterhouseCoopers LLP). 2010. *Emerging Trends in Real Estate®, 2011*. Washington, DC: Urban land Institute.

United States Access Board. 2002. *ADA Accessibility Guidelines for Buildings and Facilities (ADAAG)*. Washington, DC: USAB. http://www.access-board.gov/adaag/html/adaag.htm.

Untermann, R.K. 1984. *Accommodating the Pedestrian: Adapting Towns and Neighborhoods for Walking and Bicycling*. New York: Van Nostrand Reinhold.

———. 1990. "Street Design: Reassessing the Function, Safety and Comfort of Streets for Pedestrians." In *The Road Less Traveled: Getting There by Other Means*. Boulder, CO: 11th International Pedestrian Conference.

Unwin, R. 1909. *Town Planning in Practice*. London: T. Fisher Unwin Ltd. (Reissued by Princeton Architectural Press, New York, 1994).

Van Houten, R., R.A. Retting, C.M. Farmer, J. Van Houten, and J.E.L. Malenfant. 2000. "Field Evaluation of a Leading Pedestrian Interval Signal Phase at Three Urban Intersections." *Transportation Research Record* 1734: 86–92.

Veitch, J., S. Bagley, K. Ball, and J. Salmon. 2006. "Where Do Children Usually Play? A Qualitative Study of Parents' Perceptions of Influences on Children's Active Free-Play." *Health & Place* 12 (4): 383–93.

Walsh, R. 2012. *Local Policies and Practices That Support Safe Pedestrian Environments: A Synthesis of Highway Practice*. Washington, DC: Transportation Research Board.

Wanvik, P.O. 2009. "Effects of Road Lighting: An Analysis Based on Dutch Accident Statistics, 1987–2006." *Accident Analysis & Prevention* 41 (1): 123–28.

Warburton, N.U. 2006. "U. Student Entries May Be Future TRAX Stops." *Deseret News*, January 14.

White, R. 2009. "Spreading the Green and Sharing the Wealth." *Metroscape*, Winter, pp. 27–30.

Whyte, W.H. 1980. *The Social Life of Small Urban Spaces*. New York: Project for Public Spaces.

———. 1988. *City: Rediscovering the Center*. New York: Doubleday.

Willson, R.W. 1995. "Suburban Parking Requirements: A Tacit Policy for Automobile Use and Sprawl." *Journal of the American Planning Association* 61 (1): 29–42.

Winterbottom, D. 2000. "Residual Pace Re-Evaluated." *Places* 13 (3): 40–47.

Wolch, J., M. Jerrett, K. Reynolds, R. McConnell, R. Chang, N. Dahmann, K. Brady, et al. 2011. "Childhood Obesity and Proximity to Urban Parks and Recreational Resources: A Longitudinal Cohort Study." *Health & Place* 17 (1): 207–14.

Wolf, M. 2008. "Opening Shot." *Blueprint*, April, pp. 18–19.

Wood, L., L.D. Frank, and B. Giles-Corti. 2010. "Sense of Community and Its Relationship with Walking and Neighborhood Design." *Social Science & Medicine* 70 (9): 1381–90.

Zegeer, C., W. Hunter, L. Staplin, F. Bents, R. Huey, and J. Barlow. 2010. "Safer Vulnerable Road Users: Pedestrians, Bicyclists, Motorcyclists, and Older Users." White Paper no. 5 for *Toward Zero Deaths: A National Strategy on Highway Safety*. http://safety.transportation.org/doc/web5%20Vulnerable%20Users%20White%20Paper.pdf.

Zegeer, C., C. Seiderman, P. Lagerwey, M. Cynecki, M. Ronkin, and R. Schnieder. 2002. *Pedestrian Facilities Users Guide: Providing Safety and Mobility*. Report no. FHWA-RD-102-01. Washington, DC: Federal Highway Administration.

Zegeer, C., J.R. Stewart, H.H. Huang, and P.A. Lagerwey. 2005. *Safety Effects of Marked versus Unmarked Crosswalks at Uncontrolled Locations: Final Report and Recommended Guidelines*. Report no. FHWA-HRT-04-100. Washington, DC: Federal Highway Administration.

Zhang, H., and S. Lin. 2011. "Affective Appraisal of Residents and Visual Elements in the Neighborhood: A Case Study in an Established Suburban Community." *Landscape and Urban Planning* 101 (1): 11–21.

Zhao, F., L-F Chow, M-T Li, I. Ubaka, and A. Gan. 2003. "Forecasting Transit Walk Accessibility: Regression Model Alternative to Buffer." *Transportation Research Record* 1835: 34–41.